State Barge 1733

J. D. Crace, 16, Gloucester Place,
Portman Square, W.

CEREMONIAL BARGES
ON THE RIVER THAMES

CEREMONIAL BARGES ON THE RIVER THAMES

A History of the Barges of the City of London Livery Companies and of the Crown

KENNETH NICHOLLS PALMER

UNICORN PRESS
LONDON

Unicorn Press
21 Afghan Road
London SW11 2QD

Published by Unicorn Press 1997
Copyright © Kenneth Nicholls Palmer 1997

A catalogue record for this book is available
from the British Library

ISBN 0 906290 17 1

Designed by Mick Keates.
Formatting by Concise Artisans.
Colour separating by John Rawlinson.

Printed in Italy by Manfrini R.
Arti Grafiche Vallagarina SpA

ENDPAPERS: *William Kent's designs for Frederick Prince of Wales's Barge, 1732*

HALF TITLE PAGE: *Thames Wherries, Richmond. From E.W. Cooke,*
Shipping and Craft, London, 1829

TITLE PAGE: *Detail from Canaletto's painting of the Thames on Lord Mayor's Day c.1747.*
The City Barge appears immediately behind the sloop firing a salute.
Four livery company barges can also be seen heading upriver to Westminster,
accompanied by a large array of watermen's wherries.

CONTENTS

ACKNOWLEDGMENTS

This book could not have been completed without the help of a large number of people. When the idea to research Livery Barges first arose, I had no idea that Royalty and the Lord Mayor would become involved. I have received support from Her Majesty's Household which has included: the Private Secretary to the Queen, The Rt Hon. Sir Robert Fellowes; the Comptroller, Lt Col. W.H.M. Ross; the Queen's Bargemaster, Mr R. Crouch; the Assistant to the Surveyor of the Queen's Pictures, Mr Charles Noble; the Curator of Historic Palaces, Dr Simon Thurley; the Curator of the Royal Photograph Collection, Miss Frances Dimond. I am very fortunate in that the Lord Mayor in the year the work was completed, the Past Master of the Worshipful Society of Apothecaries, the Rt Hon. Sir John Chalstrey, has agreed to write the preface.

The main section of the book discusses the Livery Companies' barges. All those Livery Companies in existence before 1856, when the processions on the Thames ceased, have been approached, including two Companies without Livery. The Masters, past Masters, Clerks, Archivists and Beadles have been of great assistance and have put up with my ceaseless enquiries with great tolerance. All those with any connection with the ownership or hiring of barges have, I believe, been included and I am most grateful for all their help; especially Lt Col. Richard Stringer, Clerk of my own Company, Major Charles O'Leary, Archivist, and the staff of Apothecaries' Hall. It is impossible to list every one by name who has assisted in my research. However, special mention must be made of Miss Penelope Fussell, Archivist to the Drapers' Company, who has been an inspiration and a mine of information. Without her help the book would never have been anything but a collection of notes. I must also pay tribute to Dr Helen Bradley, Historian, and Miss Elizabeth Salmon, Archivist, of the Saddlers' Company who helped to form the historical background; Mrs Edwina Ehrman and Miss Hazel Forsyth of the Museum of London; Mr R.R. Aspinall, Librarian at the Docklands Museum; Mr James R. Sewell, City Archivist, and the Corporation of London Record Office; The Guildhall Library and Manuscripts Department; the Librarian, Society of Antiquaries, Fairholt Collection; Mr Colin White, Curator, and Miss Assunta Del Priore, Assistant Curator, of the Royal Naval Museum, Portsmouth; the Oxford University Archivist, the City of Oxford Archivist, The Librarian of University College and Dr W. Parry of Oriel College; the Keeper of the Archives, Queen's College; the Assistant Archivist, Christ Church; Mr David Sherriff of the Thames and Kennet Marina, Sonning; Mr John Wolstenholm of University College; Mr Norman Dix, retired College boatman; The National Maritime Museum; The Textile Conservation Centre, Hampton Court Palace; The Environment Agency, Thames Region; Miss Sarah Medlam, Deputy Curator, The Victoria and Albert Museum; Miss Heather Creaton, Deputy Director, Institute of Historical Research, University of London; Dr Robin Darwall-Smith, Centre for Oxfordshire Studies; Chris Roberts; David and Nora Scrutton; Ken Hylton-Smith; John Cox; Richard Norton; Jane Palmer; Dr J.R. Piggott, Archivist, Dulwich College. All of these people, in some measure, helped to complete a picture of the great ceremonies which took place on the Thames in the past and to determine those artefacts from the barges that have survived to this day.

Preparation of the text for publication has been facilitated by Miss Penelope Fussell, Miss Elizabeth Salmon, Mr Charles Hacon and Mr Timothy Burslem.

The generous financial assistance of a number of Livery Companies and individuals has helped to make this publication possible.

Finally, I must acknowledge the great patience and tolerance of my wife in giving up two rooms of a very small bungalow for me to work in, what appeared to her to be utter chaos for three or more years.

Illustration Acknowledgments

The author and producers of this book would like to thank all those who have given permission for pictures to be reproduced here

The Royal Collection © Her Majesty The Queen   12
British Medical Association   15
British Architectural Library, RIBA, London   endpapers
Chelsea Reference Library   161
City of London Corporation   23
Governors of Dulwich College   8
Drapers' Company   cover, 30
Manchester Metropolitan
   Borough of Bury   9
B.T. Batsford Ltd   167
Goldsmiths' Company   2
The Informer   184
The Lord Chamberlain   17
Mr David Sherriff   152-4, 159
Mr Kellaway, Blue Boar, Poole   96
Illustrated London News   16, 22, 23
Mr Paul King   154 (lower)
London Borough of Richmond upon Thames   166-7
Leander Club   163
Mr Turk of Turk's Boatyard   158 (upper)
Museum of London   15, 19 (upper), 21 (lower), 22 (upper),
   23, 24, 140
National Maritime Museum, Greenwich   11 (upper),
   13 (lower), 14
The Roudnice Lobkowicz Foundation, Prague   title pages
The Master and Fellows of Oriel College, Oxford   155, 156
The Master and Fellows of Magdalene College, Cambridge
   (Pepys Library)   21 (upper)
Royal Naval Museum, Portsmouth   10
Society of Antiquaries, Fairholt Collection   4, 20 (upper),
   67 (lower)
Royal and Sunalliance Insurance Group   148-9 (lower)
Textile Conservation Centre, Hampton Court   68
The Transport Museum (on loan from the Museum of London)
   146-7
David and Nora Scrutton   164
Oxfordshire County Archives   158
Master and Fellows of University College, Oxford   152-4
Mercers' Company   25

PREFACE

Alderman Sir John Chalstrey MA, MD, DSc, FRCS

All who are interested in London and the River Thames will be fascinated by this book, which has been conscientiously researched, delightfully written and beautifully illustrated by Kenneth Nicholls Palmer.

It is an eminently readable history of the Royal Barges and those of the City of London, which had their heyday during those centuries when travel by river was usually quicker, safer and more comfortable than along the narrow, dirty and crowded streets of the capital.

The author records what is known of these elegant craft, their designers, builders and owners as well as the purposes for which they were used. Sadly, very few of the barges survived until the end of the nineteenth century and many of their accoutrements have also disappeared. However, those artefacts which survived have been painstakingly sought out by Kenneth Nicholls Palmer, who has catalogued and photographed them for posterity. It is a task for which present and future historians will be grateful to him.

John Chalstrey

Lord Mayor of London 1995-6

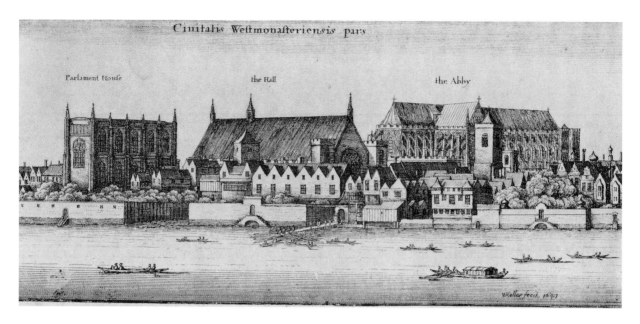

Part of Westminster, with Parliament House, Westminster Hall, and
the Abbey, from the River. *An etching by Wenceslaus Hollar, 1647.*
Westminster Stairs, the only public point of access to Westminster from the
Thames at this time, are shown in the river front

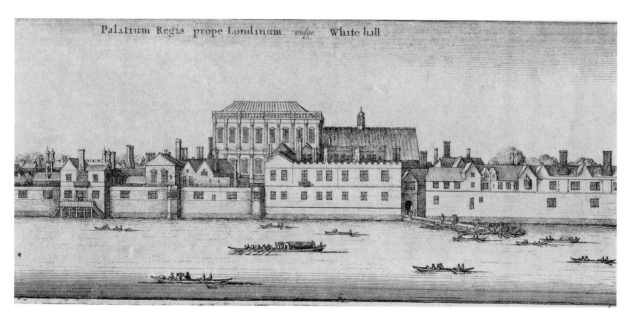

Whitehall from the River. *The Palace of Whitehall, with the Banqueting House in the cen-*
tre, seen from near the Lambeth shore of the river. An etching by Wenceslaus Hollar, 1647.
Whitehall Stairs on the right was the main entrance to the palace from the river.
A public thoroughfare ran from there through the palace to King Street

INTRODUCTION

Upon Westminster Bridge
William Wordsworth 3rd September, 1802

Earth has not anything to show more fair:
Dull would he be of soul who could pass by
A sight so touching in its majesty:
This City now doth like a garment wear
The beauty of the morning: silent, bare,
Ships, towers, domes, theatres, and temples lie
Open unto the fields, and to the sky,
All bright and glittering in the smokeless air.
Never did sun more beautifully steep
In his first splendour valley, rock, or hill;
Ne'er saw I, never felt, a calm so deep!
The river glideth at his own sweet will:
Dear God! the very houses seem asleep;
And all that mighty heart is lying still!

LIVERY BARGES at this time still had over fifty years left in which to process on the River Thames in all their splendour. Wordsworth may have seen them a number of times. Like all great cities standing on the banks of a navigable river, London owes most of its wealth and importance to its position on the Thames. In the days of commercial sailing ships, London became one of the greatest cities in the world for trade and commerce. The river gave ready access by boat to property on its banks at a time when the roads were rough and dangerous. Most of the Royal Palaces and stately homes were close to the river, hence the Royal Barges, the barges of the Livery Companies, the private shallops and many hired rowing boats. One of these small boats was hired by Pepys in 1662 at the great expense of 5*s* to watch the procession of Queen Catherine on her arrival in London to marry Charles II.

Until the roads were widened and paved, the Thames formed the main highway of the City. In the early days there were no pavements or side-walks and in winter the mud was quite a problem. People wore pattens to keep their shoes clean, which they left by the door before entering a house. Drainage was almost non-existent and a great deal of rubbish tended to collect. Travel by a small rowing boat was far cleaner and much more comfortable. Also until the early eighteenth century there was only one bridge, London Bridge, which during the day was often crowded with people, carts and animals. It was therefore usually quicker to cross the river, when necessary, by boat. Processions and pageants taking place on the river formed a great spectacle for the public, who would have a good view from the bank. This would be much better than standing in a crowded street for a procession on land. The opening of Westminster Bridge in 1750 was an event of considerable importance; it broke the City's monopoly of cross-river traffic and reduced

St Paul's and Blackfriars Bridge, *by David Roberts*

the number of watermen ferrying passengers across the river. Improved access to the City helped trade and more shipping used the port.

My interest in the Livery barges of the City of London began over five years ago when for the first time I took the opportunity to study the banners on display at Apothecaries' Hall. Initial research into the provenance of these banners, their decoration and use, and the realisation that the Apothecaries still possess other artefacts known to have been used on their barge, led me to enquire of other Livery Companies what treasures they might have that were associated with barges they had owned or hired. The primary purpose of my research was to trace and record all such treasures whether they be banners, streamers, bargemaster badges, carvings, clothing or other items known to have been associated with the barges. Many have been lost or were damaged by enemy action during the Second World War; many too had been misidentified, or their significance had not been realised. During my research some items were discovered that had been forgotten for many years. It was my intention to record as many objects as possible before they too disappeared. Photographs of artefacts that were used in connection with the barges or were of a type similar to those that were used by other Companies have been included in the illustrations.

Livery Companies played a vital part in developing trade in the City and were fundamental in establishing the position of the City of London as a centre of commercial activity. They had developed from the Mysteries and Guilds of the Middle Ages. These were originally associations for the regulation of trade, wages and standards of craftsmanship. They trained apprentices to the highest possible standard – as it was important to protect their craft from those who were unskilled – and also cared for their members in times of sickness and hardship. Members of the Companies had the right to wear special distinctive clothes or 'livery' (this being otherwise forbidden by a statute of Edward IV in 1468) – hence the name Liverymen.

The Mayor, later on the Lord Mayor, was elected from members of the Companies. In earlier years the Mayor was selected only from members of the 'Great Twelve' Companies and worthy candidates from other Companies had to 'translate' to become a member of one of these. The Companies are proud of their position in the order of 'precedence', an order initially laid down by custom and agreement, rather than by the dates of establishment of the Companies. There were disputes between the Companies regarding their relative positions on several occasions, and the 'order' was finally settled by a Court of Aldermen in 1516. In this book the Companies appear in that order.

Most of the Companies owned or hired barges at some time, usually when a Liveryman became Lord Mayor or one of the Sheriffs. This was so that they could participate in the annual procession by water to Westminster where the Lord Mayor and Sheriffs took their oaths of appointment. These processions, or Triumphs, continued until 1856. The Companies also took part in processions on the Thames on special occasions, especially when Royalty was involved. The Livery barges must have been a splendid sight decorated with flags and banners. Although the barges have long since disappeared, many of their banners and other treasures still remain and may be seen displayed in the Company Halls.

It is often forgotten that the Companies had other duties in supporting the capital city. In times of danger or the threat of invasion they helped to maintain a reserve for the Army and Navy. According to their wealth they maintained a store of weapons and they trained a number of members to use these arms. Until 150 years ago the mark of the Clothworkers' practice area for bowmen stood in a field called Shepherds and Shepherdesses, Islington. The Companies also helped to finance the building of warships, and their Livery barges were sometimes used for troop movements. In addition they were called upon for substantial loans for both King and Parliament and were required to store grain to sell to the poor when times were hard and there was a shortage of food.

The embarkation of the Lord Mayor from the Tower of London;
an early nineteenth-century view

Three Cranes Wharf in 1647 from a drawing
by Wenceslaus Hollar

One of the first records of a Company hiring a barge is in the archives of the Brewers' Company. In 1422 Sir William Walderne, a Brewer who had translated to the Mercers' Company, became Lord Mayor for the second time and processed by water to Westminster to take his oath. In the same year the Drapers hired a barge to take part in the funeral procession of Henry V. However, it was not until 1453 that the first Livery barge was built, for Sir John Norman, a Draper, to process to Westminster. It was said to be a resplendent barge, built at his own expense; afterwards he gave it to his Company together with a barge cloth, used for covering the deckhouse or cabin.

The processions to Westminster did not always start from the same place. No doubt there were reasons for this; one of the most important being the time of high water. Rowing against the tide, even with eighteen oarsmen, would have been difficult and it would have been almost imposs-ible to keep station with a large flotilla of boats. Quite often the Lord Mayor embarked from the Tower of London or Three Cranes Wharf, returning to Blackfriars to complete the procession on land by joining numerous other Companies and important citizens on his way to the Guildhall.

The Livery barges were of a similar design to a Thames wherry but very much larger. They were clinker built (with the planks overlapping, like the Viking ships) and made of seasoned timber with a long shallow bow. This was a great advantage when landing passengers on the shore, especially at low tide, as it enabled them to step on to dry land from near the bow. When the vessel was ready to leave, most of the crew went towards the stern of the boat which lifted the bow off the shore so that it was afloat again. The barges had a high or 'lute' stern, which helped the helmsman to obtain a good view of the river.

In the early years, barges had an awning to protect the passengers. Later vessels had a cabin with a flat top or 'house' to accommodate more passengers. The last barge built for the Goldsmiths' Company in 1824 had the luxury of a water closet, a great advance on the chamber pots normally used. The crew usually consisted of the Bargemaster and his mate with eighteen oarsmen. There was a small space at the stern for musicians. The overall length of the barges varied between sixty and seventy-five feet. It was not only Livery Companies who used barges but also the Crown, the Lord Mayor and other dignitaries such as the Archbishop of Canterbury, for various ceremonial occasions on the River Thames. Artefacts have survived from these barges as well. Barges were also used as vehicles of transport. They were not suitable for going to sea, as was discovered when six which had been sold to Cambridge University tried to reach Cambridge via the coast of Suffolk and Norfolk – all were wrecked.

The processions on the Thames eventually ceased in 1856. This was partly due to the cost, partly due to the increase in the number of trading vessels on the river and partly due to the great improvement in the roads. Another factor was that in 1857 the City handed over responsibility of the Thames to the new Conservancy Board. This in turn gave control of the tidal Thames to the Port of London Authority in 1909. On at least one occasion during the last few years the barges had to be towed by steam boats.

Thirty Livery Companies, which were estab-lished before processions on the Thames ceased in 1856, have been omitted from this book. These appear to have had very little connection with the river or with Livery barges. Unfortunately it has not been possible to check all their archives in full. They have all contributed to the wealth and prosperity of the City. Of these Companies the Plumbers (no. 31) were one of the ten asked to donate a banner to hang in the Guildhall in 1911; and the Glass-sellers (no. 71) possess a flag which is a nineteenth-century representation of an older banner which has not survived. There are two Companies without Livery, established before 1856, the Watermen and the Parish Clerks. Of these only the former has a history relating to barges.

THE ROYAL BARGES

ROYAL PROCESSIONS on the Thames were quite frequent during the Tudor period. Notable processions included that on the occasion of the coronation of Henry VII's Queen (Elizabeth of York) in 1487 and those in 1533 for the coronation of Anne Boleyn and later in the same year for the christening of the future Queen Elizabeth. During the reign of Henry VIII most members of the Royal family seem to have had his or her own barge as did the more important courtiers. The King owned several small 'botes' in addition to the Royal Barge. When he made an important visit by water, the Royal Barge was accompanied by 'privy botes' to carry his body-servants and wardrobe. The King's Bargemaster had the responsibility of organising this flotilla, including the provision of 'swete herbs' to burn so as to hide the offensive smells of the river. Soft furnishings too were provided for the comfort of the passengers. In 1535 repairs and maintenance of the King's Barge cost £4 2s 1d. In 1539 Henry VIII was rowed up to Lambeth Palace with drums and fifes playing.

The King's Barge was called 'Lyon'. Later Henry VIII had another Royal Barge called 'Greyhound', possibly named after the sinister supporter of his Arms (the supporters were not constant throughout his reign, in fact he changed them several times). Henry VIII made full use of his barge when he was in residence at Hampton Court. Here there was a water gate or landing place and a long gallery with a privy stair giving direct access to his privy lodging. In order to make the best use of the river, Henry had a special clock installed at Hampton Court Palace to show the time of the tide. Rowing a heavy barge against the tide would have been difficult for the oarsmen and the journey would have taken much longer. A house close to the Thames was a great help for a comfortable journey.

In 1539 there was a Royal Bargehouse just above where Blackfriars Bridge now stands, on the south side of the river. In 1540 a new dock and bargehouse were built at Whitehall for the new palace which occupied a large site close to the river. There are a number of references to a Royal Barge in the state papers, foreign and domestic, of Henry VIII. Amongst these on 30 June 1538, John Johnson, Master of the King's Barge, was paid 10s for burning and tallowing the Great Barge. Later the same year he was paid 2s and twenty-four men were each given 12 pence for rowing the King between London and Greenwich both ways. On 25 November 1539, £29 4s was paid for building a new barge with twenty-four oars. Fortunately the remains of the water gate and landing steps of Whitehall Palace, built by Henry VIII, have been preserved. The Palace was once the largest royal palace in Europe.

Queen Elizabeth made good use of her barge, in preference to the rough and muddy roads with open drains, when travelling between her palaces of Greenwich, Whitehall, Richmond and Hampton Court which were all situated close to the Thames. Dulwich College is fortunate in that their founder Edward Alleyn (1556-1626) purchased part of Queen Elizabeth's Royal Barge when it was broken up. Alleyn left a written record of the purchase, which included two interesting paintings which have survived and are still in the care of Dulwich College; they are described by the Librarian Dr J.R. Piggott in *The Alleynian* Special Issue, number 636, 1976. The paintings were bought with 'all ye upper part of Queen Elizabeth's State Barge' on 19 December 1618 for £2 2s 6d. The original record of this purchase is recorded in a diary held in the College Library. The paintings are on wood framed by columns which are believed to be of the same period. They represent two female figures entitled Pietas (duty, patriotism or affection) and Liberalitas (kindness, generosity or bounty) and formed part of the decoration of the Queen's cabin.

Another reference in the College's collection is to Paul Hentzner, tutor to a young German nobleman who visited Bankside in 1598. The tutor recalled Queen Elizabeth's visit to sup with Lord Pembroke at Baynard's Castle in 1589. She travelled by barge and was observed by the Spanish Ambassador to be flirting with Leicester.

Elizabeth's Royal Bargehouse is referred to by Horace Walpole in the eighteenth century at his Strawberry Hill Press: 'Without the City are some theatres [this would include the Globe and a bear garden] . . . not far from these theatres, which were built of wood, lies the Royal Barge, close to the river. It has two cabins, beautifully ornamented with glass windows, painting and gilding. It is kept on dry ground and sheltered from the weather.' The site is marked on an Ordnance Survey Map dated 1872, close to Barge House Alley up river of Blackfriars Bridge on the Lambeth side of the Thames. It is shown as the King's Bargehouse. The area is now covered by new buildings and a new river wall with a footpath. As recently as the nineteen-fifties, the landing place could be located at low tide by some old oak piles with iron bands.

Pageants on the water were also very much the fashion during the reign of James I and Charles II. A number of Royal Barges must have been built; fortunately three of these remain. The oldest is believed to have been built for Charles II. It is now in the Royal Naval Museum at

Portsmouth and is in excellent condition. This barge (or more correctly shallop) is 35ft long with a 6ft 1in beam. It was last used in January 1806 to carry Lord Nelson's body from Greenwich to Whitehall for his state funeral. The shallop was draped over the sides and canopy with black material. The crew were suitably clothed in mourning. The procession was probably the largest ever to take place on the Thames, with over sixty vessels including the barges of the Lord Mayor and eight Livery Companies.

A shallop built in 1689 for Queen Mary, wife of William III, was 41ft long, clinker built with sockets for a portable canopy, and had eight oarsmen. It was used by George V and Queen Mary in 1912 for a Royal Regatta at Henley. In 1918 it was used for a Royal occasion at Eton, and in 1919 it was used for the last time for a Peace Pageant. The barge, or shallop, is now exhibited in the National Maritime Museum at Greenwich.

In 1732 a barge, or shallop, was built for Frederick, Prince of Wales, by John Hall. It was designed by William Kent with decoration carved by James Richards. It is a fine craft, 63ft long and 7ft wide with a small cabin or house 7ft long. Later this barge was used by a succession of monarchs. Its last appearance afloat was for the opening of the Coal Exchange in 1849 when the Bargemaster wore a black velvet cap and the oarsmen fur caps. It is now exhibited at Greenwich. The National Maritime Museum also has two eighteenth-century barges which belonged to the Commissioners of the Navy.

Prince Albert, acting on behalf of Queen Victoria, and accompanied by the Prince of Wales and the Princess Royal, used the Queen's State Barge to process from Whitehall Steps for the opening of the Coal Exchange. On this occasion twenty-two of the Queen's Watermen rowed the barge under the charge of Mr Roberts of Lambeth, the Queen's Bargemaster. They were attired in scarlet uniforms with gold badges and black velvet caps. This must have been the last use of such a large Royal Barge. The Queen's shallop rowed by eight oarsmen was also present containing state officers of the royal household. This occasion is fully described in the *Illustrated London News* of 3 November 1849.

The Queen still has a Royal Bargemaster and Royal Watermen hold office under him. The Royal Bargemaster is on duty when the Queen is attending ceremonies on the Thames. He also has other duties which have survived from the days when more use was made of the Thames for carrying passengers and cargo. One of these duties is to ensure the safe transport from Buckingham Palace of the crown for a coronation and for the Queen to wear at the opening of Parliament. There are still five Bargemasters who have duties on the Thames, of whom the Queen's Bargemaster is the senior. The other four are the Fishmongers' who has duties with the races for the Doggett's Coat and Badge; and the Vintners', the Dyers' and the Watermen's who together are responsible with the Queen's Bargemaster for Swan Upping, the annual marking of young swans belonging to the Monarch, the Vintners and the Dyers, who are the only people allowed to own swans on the River Thames. For the duties of Swan Upping these gentlemen are known as Swan Markers. Members of the Watermen's Company provide the crew when required.

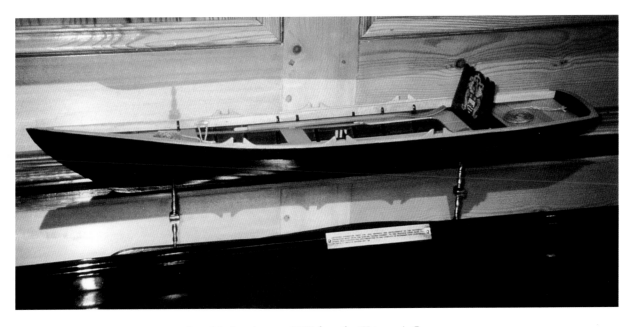

A model of a wherry c. 1800 from the Watermen's Company

Two painted panels from the cabin of Queen Elizabeth I's Barge,
with (below) evidence of the purchase by Edward Alleyn,
founder of Dulwich College, for £2 2s 6d in 1618

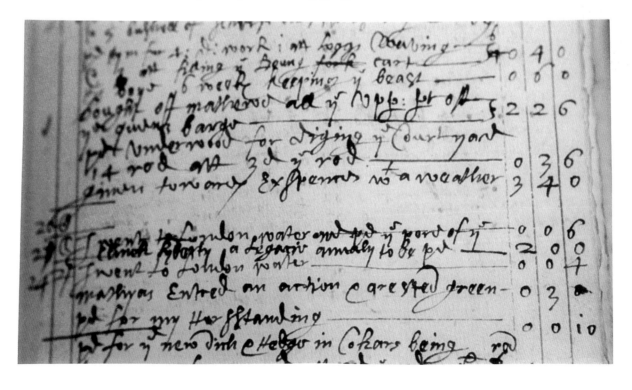

The remains of the water gate of Whitehall Palace,
built by Henry VIII

The Happier Days of Charles I by Frederick Goodall

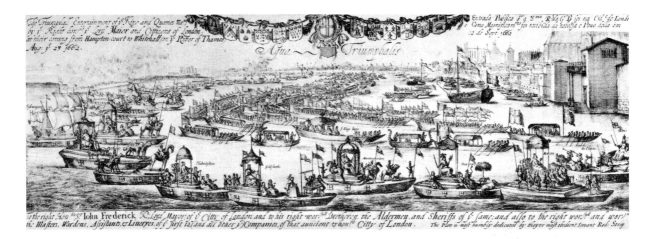

*A royal procession from Hampton Court to Whitehall. One of
seven engravings by Roderick Stoop, commemorating the reception
of Catherine of Braganza, 23rd August 1662. (Note the two
gondolas which had been presented to the King the previous year)*

*The Royal Barge of Charles II exhibited at the
Royal Naval Museum at Portsmouth*

*Charles II's barge being used for the funeral procession
of Lord Nelson*

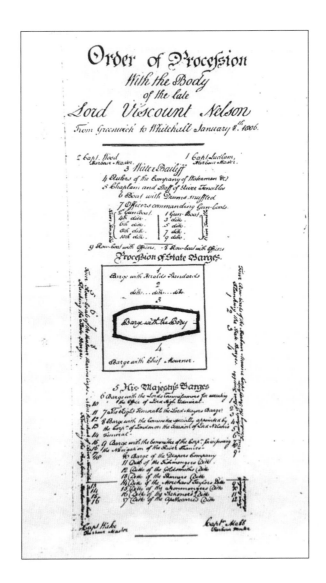

*Queen Mary and the Prince of Wales leaving Whitehall steps
in a hurry at the time of her husband James II's abdication,
19th December 1688*

*Queen Mary's shallop at Henley in 1912 with George V and
Queen Mary. By the gracious permission of HM the Queen*

King George V landing at Cadogan Pier from Queen Mary's
shallop after the Peace Procession in 1919

Queen Mary's shallop exhibited at
The National Maritime Museum, Greenwich

Detail of the splendid carving on the stern of
Prince Frederick's Royal Barge

'Royal Aquatic Excursion', a paper cut-out toy of c.1843 published by Dean & Co., shows Queen Victoria and Prince Albert with their children in the barge built for Frederick, Prince of Wales by John Hall in 1732

Royal Bargeman, 1843

THE QUEEN'S BARGE.

This splendid house-barge or galley, which has recently been undergoing a thorough repair at her Majesty's dockyard, Deptford, was built for George II. when Prince of Wales. Her length is 64 feet, and her breadth 6 feet, 8 inches. She is double-banked ; manned by twelve oars, and the house will conveniently hold from twelve to fourteen persons. The last important occasion upon which she was employed was the funeral of the immortal Nelson, whose remains were conveyed in her from Greenwich to London.

Since that period she has been laid up in the boat-house at Deptford, and narrowly escaped being sold a short time since in consequence of an order being received from the Admiralty to dispose of the unemployed small craft. In consequence, however, of the report of the master boat-builder at Woolwich dockyard, of her superior build and decorations, orders were immediately given for preparing her for the Queen. The whole of the carvings are in oak, and of the most superb workmanship. She is now being gilded, and her destination, when completed, is Virginia Water.

An account of the restoration of Frederick Prince of Wales's Barge
from the Illustrated London News *of 20th July 1842*

Queen Victoria's Royal Barge with 22 oarsmen at the opening
of the Coal Exchange by Prince Albert on 3rd November 1849
(Illustrated London News)

The Queen's Bargemaster, Mr Robert Crouch, receiving the Crown from Lt. Col. W.H.M. Ross, following the opening of Parliament

Part of the Bargemaster's uniform

THE LORD MAYOR AND THE CITY BARGES

THE OFFICE of Mayor or Chief Citizen of London dates back to 1189. The Mayor was virtually the ruler of the City. Until 1857 the Lord Mayor had control over the navigation of the Thames and the Port of London and surveyed the river at regular intervals. A Water Bailiff was responsible to the Mayor and reported to the Court of Common Council at regular intervals. The 1799 Bailiff's salary was £500; he had five assistants. The Lord Mayor was Admiral of the Port of London and entitled to be piped aboard vessels of HM Navy as an Officer of Flag Rank.

At first barges had to be hired for an inspection of the river by the Mayor, as well as for ceremonial duties. In 1495 a 'fair barge' was to be trimmed for the Lord Mayor to receive the Great Admiral and other Noblemen from France. In 1512 a barge was to be provided for the Lord Mayor and the Aldermen to go to Syon. About the same time the Chamberlain was to provide a boat for the Mayor and Sheriffs to proceed to Westminster to take their oaths of appointment. In February 1662 the Water Bailiff had permission to make three persons free of the City to defray the charges of an eight-oared barge.

A barge must have been built for the City by the middle of the seventeenth century, because in 1671 there are bills for repairing a City Barge. An interesting account, dated October 1687, survives giving details of carving by Jonathan Maine for a new barge: 'The King's Arms £7, 4 large dragons £9, 41 foot of shields and festoons £24, 2 trail boards £7 10s, the City Arms and supporters for the stern £9 10s, festoons of flowers £3 10s, two large dolphins on stern £3 10s, elm timber £5 10s; total £79 10s'. Another account dated 1687 is for nineteen silver badges for the crew and the mate, ordered by the Water Bailiff from Frances Garthorne at a cost of £48 4d, less the value of the old badges £31 14s. With this bill is another for launching the new City Barge for 30s. In the same year a tilt was ordered

to be made for the eight-oared barge. In 1711 an eighteen-oared City Barge was built for ceremonial duties such as escorting Royalty and meeting important visitors. It is apparent from the accounts that the City owned at least three barges of differing sizes for various purposes.

Later bills have more details and give a clear indication of the decorative and sumptuous nature of the barges. In 1773 the painting and gilding of the new barge is described in full. The following year Henry Fletcher, upholsterer of Tower Street, submitted an account for twenty-six crimson silk Damask curtains, thirteen cushions of crimson cloth with silk tufts, sixteen sash strings and a mat, baize coverings for the images and carved work all at a cost of £95 7s 6d.

The last Livery type barge belonging to the City, which had been built in 1807, was sold by auction in 1860 for £85, four years after the last procession by the Lord Mayor to Westminster. Sir Matthew Wood, Lord Mayor in 1815 and 1816, commissioned an additional barge to be built in 1815 which he named after his daughter *Maria Wood*. This barge was very much larger than any of the Livery barges or the 1807 City Barge, being 140ft long × 19ft beam, with a draught of 2ft 6ins. She could only move on her own by working the tides with six watermen using sweeps and long poles. Up river where there was a tow path she could be pulled by six horses. On a few occasions she was towed by a steam boat. After his second year as Lord Mayor, Sir Matthew Wood presented the barge to the City. She was present at the opening of the new London Bridge by William IV in 1831. In 1859 she was sold by the City; later she was hired by the Butchers' Company. Finally, the *Maria Wood* became a pile-driver barge and was broken up in 1920.

The archives of the City are held in the Record Office of the Corporation of London. Additional minutes from 1770-1857 can be examined at the Docklands branch of the Museum of London at Poplar.

*A model of the last City barge, made by the builders,
showing the lute stern and transom*

*A replica of the City Bargemaster's badge
made by Philip Rundell in 1828*

The Lord Mayor landing at Westminster at low tide c.1846

The Lord Mayor, Sir John Key Bt, Stationer, in the The Lord Mayor's
barge at the opening of new London Bridge in 1831

An engraving of the Lord Mayor's barge in 1676

The Maria Wood, *the last City barge, overall 140 feet*

A peajacket belonging to one of the crew of the City Barge

*The embarkation of the Lord Mayor at Oxford
for a survey of the river, 15 August 1846*

THE EMBAR

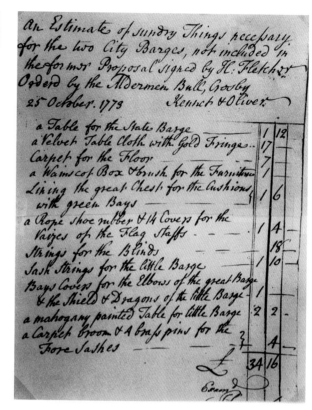

The bill of Mr Hall, shipwright, for building the 18-oared City barge in 1722

An estimate which includes items for the great City barge and the little barge in 1773

OXFORD.

THE MERCERS' COMPANY is the premier Livery Company in the City of London and as such has played a major part in the history of the City, particularly in developing trade overseas. Originally a medieval guild which existed to regulate mercantile trade and to provide a fraternity for its membership, since the sixteenth century it has been more involved in the management of property and charities entrusted to its care by benefactors, notably Richard (Dick) Whittington, John Colet (Dean of St. Paul's), Sir Thomas Gresham and Henry Howard the Earl of Northampton.

The Company's first Charter was granted by Richard II in 1394, probably through the agency of Richard Whittington. Unlike most of the Livery Companies, the Mercers did not have an early grant of Arms. However, they were granted a common seal showing a maid's head. This symbol was displayed on their property and can still be seen on a number of buildings in the City. In 1568 the College of Arms registered the seal as the Company Arms. The Arms depict a figure wearing a crimson robe adorned with gold, her neck encircled by a jewelled necklace, wearing a gold crown and a garland of roses, ascending from a bank of clouds. In 1911 a confirmation of Arms formally granted the Company a crest and motto 'honor deo'. There is no clue as to the maid's identity. Theories include one that she represents the Virgin Mary, another that she was borrowed from a contemporary tavern sign or finally that she represents an end-product of the Mercer's trade – fine clothing.

As the Mercers had eighty-five Lord Mayors before the processions to Westminster ceased on the Thames in 1856, they must have been represented afloat on a number of occasions, either in their own barge or using a hired barge. One of the first references to a hired barge was by the bachelors (or freemen) who were to attend Sir Ralph Verney, Mercer, Lord Mayor in 1465. On this occasion the bachelors wore violet gowns with scarlet hoods. The Company owned four barges, built in 1632, 1657, 1671 and 1718. There are very full details of these barges in the archives held at Mercers' Hall, particularly for the one built in 1671. The Company had their own bargehouse at Vauxhall from 1642 to 1867. It shared this property with the Fishmongers and the Clothworkers. The Apothecaries built a barge in 1673, the exact copy of the Mercers' 1671 barge. The original sketch of the last Company barge, built in 1718, appears to be the only drawing of a barge of this type and period in existence.

The Company does not possess any barge flags or banners and unfortunately the Bargemaster's badge has not survived. New banners were ordered in 1701, one with the Arms of the Lord Mayor elect, Sir William Gore, and seven Company banners. The figure of the Virgin Mary was to be taken out of the preat or long flag and replaced by the Company's Arms, at a cost of £6. On Lord Mayor's Day, the Company embarked at Three Cranes Wharf for Westminster. On their return Sir William was saluted by artillery. It is also recorded that four gilded figures carved by Richard Cleare to decorate the barge were stolen when it was sold. Unfortunately there is no description of these figures.

In spite of Mercers' Hall being completely destroyed during the Second World War, it still has many treasures including the Charter of Elizabeth I dated 1560, a seventeenth-century carving of the Mercers' Maid and an early sixteenth-century statue of Christ. The statue was discovered beneath the floor of the site of Mercers' Chapel in 1954 during the building of the third Mercers' Hall. Nearly all the Livery Companies are associated with a local church. However, the Mercers' Company is the only Company which still has a chapel of its own in regular use, although the Merchant Taylors have a small well-preserved twelfth-century chapel in a crypt.

*A seventeenth-century carving of the Arms of the
Mercers' Company from their chapel*

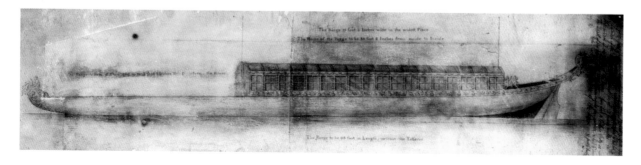

The design for the Mercer's fourth barge, 1718

THE GROCERS' COMPANY (2)

THE GROCERS' COMPANY was originally known as the Guild of Pepperers; its records date from 1180. It was a religious and social fraternity of merchants trading in spices, gold and other luxury goods from Byzantium and the Mediterranean. Pepper was valuable and often used as currency, hence the term 'peppercorn rent'. Like other guilds and Companies their community was centred on a local church, in this case the Church of St Antonin. They were involved in the import and export of all kinds of goods, which were traded 'in gross' and eventually changed their name to Grossers. Until the time of the Great Fire, they were in control of the weights of goods imported or exported through the Port of London and had charge of the King's Beam, the standard measurement of weight.

The Grocers' first Royal Charter was granted in 1428. Arms were granted in 1532 depicting a red chevron between nine cloves with a crest of a bridled camel carrying on his back two bags of pepper powdered with cloves and corded. The camel represents their trade with the East; the cloves and pepper bags allude to the union of the Spicers and Pepperers in 1429. Two griffins were added as supporters in 1532 along with the motto 'God grant grace'.

The Grocers must have taken part in a number of processions on the Thames, thirty-eight of their Livery becoming Lord Mayor before the Livery barges ceased to be used on the Thames. The Grocers' earliest surviving records commence in 1428, the first few pages being written on skin. The first reference to a barge in their archives is in 1451: it was hired for a procession on the Thames to Westminster when Mathew Phylip and Christopher Warter, members of the Company, were the two Sheriffs. The cost was 7s. In the following year Richard Lee and Richard Alley, also members, were elected as Sheriffs and a barge was hired for 7s. Richard Lee went on to become Mayor in 1460, when again another barge was probably hired. On the same page in the accounts there are two entries, undated, for the hire of one barge to Westminster for 'kynges Dirge and on the morwe to the mass . . .' – which cost 8s 6d on the first occasion and 9s 9d on the second. In 1454, when Richard Lee was Master, an inventory was recorded – headed In the Great Chamber – which includes one Great Standard, seventeen banners with Arms for trumpets, and other banners. Also 'Item 1 long telde Steyned for ye bachelers barge'.

There must have been other barges, owned or hired. There are good details of the rebuilding of the Company barge in March 1760 at the cost of £180. Painting and gilding the barge and images by Robert Moss cost a further £110. In 1805 there was an estimate for a new barge by Richard Roberts for £1,880. In August 1806 there is an estimate of £110 from George Taylor, the York Herald, for making colours for Charles II the first King of England who was of the Company; the colours to be borne as a mark of antiquity in preference to the present Royal Arms. Also in the archives is a reference to leasing a bargehouse at Lambeth from His Grace the Archbishop of Canterbury in 1805 for a rental of 10s and 11s 3d land tax per year for twenty-one years.

The Grocers' barge is listed by the Watermens' Company as taking part in three processions to Westminster: in 1780 when Sir Watkin Lewes, Joiner, was Lord Mayor and there were sixteen barges taking part; in 1828 when William Thompson, Ironmonger, was Lord Mayor, and there were nine Livery barges together with the Swan Cutter, the Thames Navigation Shallop, a shallop with a band and the Water Bailiff's craft (the Vintners' barge was the first Livery barge as it belonged to the ex Lord Mayor); and in 1843, when Sir William Magnay, Stationer, was Lord Mayor, there were twelve barges.

The last Company barge, having fallen into disrepair, was sold in 1845. Unfortunately no flags, banners or carved figures have survived but the Company is fortunate to have its Bargemaster's Badge dated 1759. The badge was nearly lost when the Bargemaster's coat was about to be destroyed in 1889. It did not appear to be silver and the Beadle considered that it was of no value. It was given to the Junior Clerk, who eventually sold it to a jeweller. Some time later a jeweller in Cheapside brought it to the notice of the Company and it was re-purchased. A large carving of a griffin adorned the Grocers' barge on ceremonial occasions and was included in an inventory for 1452. A contemporary sketch for the Arms on the stern of one of the Grocers' Company barges was found recently at the Goldsmiths' Hall.

The Arms of the Grocers' Company in wrought iron

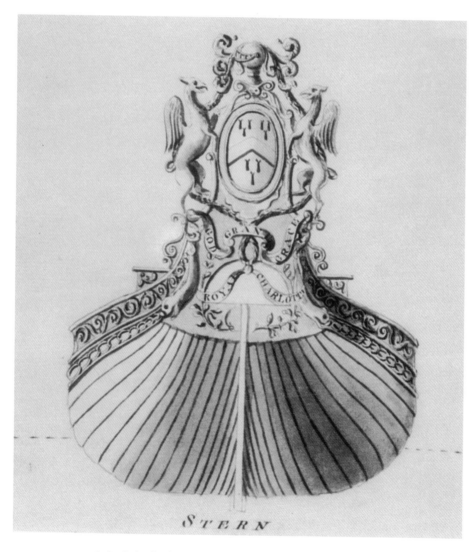

A sketch for the design of the stern of the Grocers' Company Barge

The Grocers' Bargemaster's badge 1759

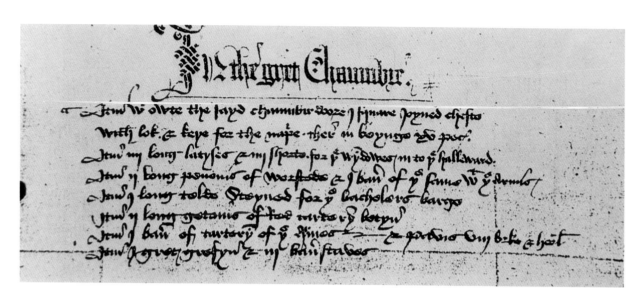

An inventory taken in 1454 which mentions 'the Great Griffen',
a carved figure carried on the Grocers' barge

Details from the archives of the costs of barge hire
to Westminster for two sheriffs in 1452

THE DRAPERS' COMPANY originated as a fraternity (the Guild of the Blessed Virgin Mary of Drapers of London) regulating the buying and selling of cloth within the City. With the expansion of the English woollen and cloth trade it became prosperous and one of the wealthiest of the guilds. Over the centuries its connections with the cloth trade ceased and today its main function is the administration of charitable trusts.

The Company received its first Charter from Edward III in 1364. It was incorporated in 1438 and in the following year received its Grant of Arms which is the earliest surviving English grant to a corporate body. The Arms depict three clouds from which issue sunbeams and which are crowned with triple crowns. The crest depicting a ram and the pelleted lions as supporters were granted in 1560; the motto 'Unto God only be honour and glory' was granted in 1613. The triple crowns represent the Company's patron saint, the Blessed Virgin Mary.

The Company has had over seventy Mayors and thus would have participated in a number of river processions. Henry Fitz Alwyn, the first Mayor of London in 1189, is believed to have been a Draper. It appears that John Walcot, a Draper, and John Love were the first to hire a barge to travel to Westminster by water as Sheriffs to take their oaths in 1389. John Walcot became Lord Mayor in 1402. The Drapers too hired a barge to take part in the funeral procession of Henry V in 1422, and again in 1429 at a cost of 3s 8d, when Henry VI was crowned at Westminster. The Wardens' accounts for the 1430s contain several references to the hire of a barge at a cost of 5s.

In 1453 the Mayor, Sir John Norman, a Draper, became the first to have a special barge built though it is unclear whether or not the Drapers' Company was given the use of Norman's barge after 1453. There are references in the Company's archives to a barge used at the procession for Elizabeth of York's coronation in 1486 and again in 1521 when watermen's uniforms were provided for those who rowed the barge. In 1533, when Sir Christopher Askew was Lord Mayor, the Drapers were without a barge and hired the great barge of the Archbishop of Canterbury with its twenty-eight oars and cushions for the passengers. In 1540, when Sir William Roche was Lord Mayor, they hired the *Greyhound*, the royal barge of Henry VIII.

A Company barge was built in 1614 for the mayoralty of Sir Thomas Davies. Another was built in time for the restoration of Charles II which cost £90. The watermen who rowed the new barge were given new coats of blue cloth sewn with the Company's insignia; six small banners and six small streamers were also ordered. The Company was thus well equipped to escort Catherine of Braganza on the occasion of her marriage to Charles in 1662. Further barges were built in 1683, 1715 and 1733 for which there are extensive details in the archives at Drapers' Hall.

The 1715 barge, built by shipwright John Loftus, was 65ft 6in long and the house 27ft 6in long. In 1733 something larger was required so John Hall built the new barge 74ft long with a house that was 33ft in length. This barge was richly carved, painted and gilded. Hall charged £315 exclusive of the painting and gilding for a barge made of 'English white growing oak timber'. A large shield carved with the Company's arms was incorporated at the stern; a figure of the Blessed Virgin Mary flanked by two angels adorned the bulkhead; and sea nymphs appeared aft. In the house, fitted with thirty-six panes of glass, the King's arms were carved above the Master's chair (the rest of the Company sat on forms). Festoons, Corinthian capitals and a

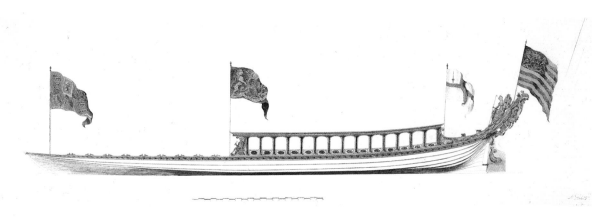

An unexecuted design by Richard Roberts for the Drapers' State Barge, 1780

carved ram added to the decorative effect. The bottom of the barge lasted thirty years, the house longer. When the renovations took place the Court gave the old hull to the Bargemaster 'as encouragement to his career'.

By 1779 the Company's barge was in a state of disrepair. Richard Roberts submitted a design for a new barge. However, this was never built; instead George Searle, who had been looking after the Company's barge for several years, was commissioned for a new bottom and repairs to the house which cost £480 plus £20 for extra carving. The renovated barge lasted well. It was used for the funeral of Lord Nelson on which occasion the Drapers' barge led the other seven City Company barges because Nelson had been an honorary freeman of the Drapers' Company.

The last Draper Lord Mayor, John Thomas Thorp, elected in 1820, enjoyed the traditional river procession to Westminster in the City barge accompanied by the Drapers' barge. The barge also took part in the last river entertainment held in 1828 to commemorate the Battle of Waterloo. The lease of the bargehouse at Lambeth was due to expire in 1831. This brought the future of the barge into question and it was decided that it should be sold. In 1829 the barge and all its fitting were sold for £35 – an estimated £180 was saved in running expenses. The Drapers' lease included accommodation for the bargemaster, who may have retired at the same time.

Among the Company's extant treasures are the badges of the Bargemaster and the oarsmen. The Bargemaster's badge is dated 1671 and cost £5 8s. On its reverse are scratched the initials of various bargemasters. The twenty-two oarsmen's badges are not dated but it is probable that they are those bought in 1792 when James Sanderson was Lord Mayor. These badges are in the form of the Company's crest, a ram, in silver-gilt and worn on the oarsmen's caps.

The Arms of the Drapers' Company

*The Bargemaster's badge and 22 badges for the crew
of the Drapers' Barge*

THE FISHMONGERS' COMPANY is known to have been an organised community long before Edward I granted them their first Charter in 1272. No fish could be sold in London except by the Mystery of Fishmongers who ensured that none but sound fish were offered for sale. As fish was one of the chief necessities of life in the Middle Ages, the wealth and influence of the Company increased enormously. Indeed it was able to furnish three ships for the Crown during the reign of Edward I. The Company also made a substantial contribution to the cost of the Hundred Years War with France.

Sir William Walworth, Prime Warden of the Fishmongers and Mayor of London, achieved fame by killing Wat Tyler when the young Richard II appeared to be in great danger during the Peasants' Revolt. With Wat Tyler's death the rebellion fizzled out. Walworth's dagger is preserved in Fishmongers' Hall. The Company lost its monopoly of the fish market in the fifteenth century, but remained concerned with fishing and retained the power to take action within Billingsgate should the food hygiene regulations be contravened.

The Fishmongers were granted their Coat of Arms in 1512, at the time of the union of the Fishmongers and the Stockfishmongers, who dealt with dried fish. The Arms depict three dolphins between two pairs of stockfish, with a crown lying over the mouth of each, and three pairs of keys of St Peter, the patron saint of the Company. The Crest depicts two arms holding an imperial crown; the supporters are a merman armed, holding in his right hand a falchion and sustaining with his left hand the helm and timber, and a mermaid holding in her left hand a mirror and supporting the Arms with her right hand. The motto reads 'All worship be to God only'.

There are two banners, painted on silk, both of the full Company Arms. One is 6ft by 12ft with a sleeve for a flag pole. The other is a banner 4ft by 6ft. The Company has a Bargemaster's Badge in excellent condition, dated 1730 and made by Robert Hall.

The Company Hall is situated at the edge of the Thames close to London Bridge. For many years it had its own wharf between the Hall and the river. The Company had over twenty Mayors after the processions commenced on the Thames and before the first Company barge was built, so they may well have hired a barge on a number of occasions. The first barge was built by Richard Mitchell for £78 in 1634. A bargemaster was hired and in 1642 a bargehouse was obtained at Vauxhall Manor close to the bargehouses of the Mercers and the Clothworkers. A second barge was built in 1662 by Henry Forty for £110, plus £28 for extras and £50 for painting and gilding. In 1691 a bargemaster was paid £110 plus £6 for new oars, £9 for special joinery, painting by M. Bird for £38 and carving by 'Mayne' for £27. The carver was probably Jonathan Maine who carved wood and stone for several of Wren's churches. The figure of St Peter, the Fishmongers' patron saint, is probably his work from the 1734 or 1773 barge. It stands in the present Hall together with an excellent scale model of the last barge built in 1773. Also in the entrance hall are two figures of angels with trumpets from the stern of the barge. The Company's last barge was broken up in the 1850s.

As with other Livery Companies, the Fishmongers took part in pageants on the Thames. Their contribution was the model of a fishing boat on a float with a cargo of fish on board. Later this same model had wheels attached and took part in the Lord Mayor's Show on land. This was popular with the poorer members of the crowd as the crew threw fish to them on the way. The term 'float' is still used for the exhibits in the Lord Mayor's show.

The bow badge from the Company barge

The Fishmongers' banner depicting the full Arms,
painted on silk approximately 6ft by 12 ft

A carved angel, one of two quarter badges

A carving of the Fishmongers' Arms from the stern
of one of their last barges

The Bargemaster's badge made by Robert Hall 1730

A portrait of Mr John Dards, bargemaster 1807-1837

A carving of St Peter, the Company's patron saint

*A funeral pall c.1500, showing Our Lord giving
the Keys of Heaven to St Peter*

The Goldsmiths' Company was first mentioned as a guild paying a fine to the Crown in 1180 and received its first Royal Charter in 1327. It had the great responsibility of regulating the standard of gold and silverware. Everything made of these precious metals had to be brought to Goldsmiths' Hall to be marked, giving rise to the term 'hallmark'. Perhaps an even greater responsibility was and still is the testing of the nation's coinage at their Assay Office. The quality of Britain's gold coins made it one of the more reliable coinages in the whole world. This must have contributed to the trade and wealth of the City and the country.

The Company was granted its Coat of Arms in 1571. A good example of these Arms can be seen over a doorway at the top of the main staircase. These are believed to be from the 1745 barge. They are quartered and depict in the first and fourth a gold leopard's head and in the second and third a covered cup between two buckles, which symbolise the union of the delegated royal privilege of assay and the trade of goldsmith respectively. The Crest depicts a demi-virgin, issuing from clouds, in a red gown and gold kirtle, with arms extended holding a balance and touchstone symbolising the Company's responsibility of assay and the Trial of the Pyx respectively. Unicorns appear as supporters and probably symbolised wealth. The motto is 'Justitia virtutum regina' (Justice is the queen of virtues).

The Company appointed a Bargemaster in Tudor times, who supplied both the barge and the watermen to propel it. In 1616 Anthony Cooper, a Liveryman, offered to give £20 towards the purchase of a barge. After some debate this offer was refused but in 1656 it was decided to commission a Company barge to be built as recent hiring had not been satisfactory. A barge was built by Edmund Tue at a cost of £100. It was to be of seasoned oak, 62ft in length, 9ft 10in beam and 2ft 11in draught, propelled by fourteen oars. A second rather larger barge was built in 1682 being 73ft in length. The barge cloth, which was embroidered, had to be extended. This covered the area for passengers. In 1687 when Sir John Shorter was Lord Mayor a barge called the *Maidenhead* had to be hired to carry additional members of the Company. The Company finances were not good in 1713 and members of the Company had shares in a third barge.

A fourth barge was built by John and Edward Hall in 1745 for the Mayoralty of Richard Hoare. There is a good description of this in the Company archives at Goldsmiths' Hall. It was 75ft 4ins in length and the barge house or cabin was 34ft. There is a list of the ornaments including a figure of St Dunstan, their patron saint who is shown with a crozier and tongs. A legend has it that when the Devil tempted him in the form of a beautiful maiden, he seized the Devil by the nose with his tongs and refused to release him until he promised never to tempt him again. Also in the list is a carving of the Company Arms, two figures of Britannia, two cups with covers and two unicorns holding shields of the Company's Arms.

A fifth barge was commissioned in 1777 and would have been ready in good time for Samuel Plumbe, Goldsmith, who was Lord Mayor in 1778. In 1824 the sixth barge was built in the year that John Garrett was Lord Mayor, and appears to have been of an improved design. The rowlocks were lowered and the oarsmen reduced from eighteen to sixteen. (The barge overtook that of the Mercers' Company's in the procession of 1835; the Mercers', being the senior Company, protested.) This barge also had a water closet and a stairway leading to an upper deck surrounded by a guard rail. The Goldsmiths used their barge for entertainment and made a number of voyages up the Thames to fashionable houses at Twickenham, Chiswick and Richmond. The barge was used for the last time in 1845 and was reputedly sold to Oriel College, Oxford, where it survived as a rowing club boat house until the 1890s.

The Company's bargehouse was initially at Lambeth where land had been purchased with the Skinners' Company next to the King's Bargehouse in 1656. The two Companies moved to the Apothecaries' property at Chelsea in 1807.

The Company still possesses several items from its barges. It has the Bargemaster's badge of silver gilt, hallmarked 1761, made by John Payne, a member of the Company, and a carving of their Arms from the cabin of their last barge. The Company also has an interesting maplewood wine bowl decorated with silver. This commemorates the birth of the future Prince of Wales, later to become Edward VII, which was announced on the day the Goldsmiths' barge was in procession up river to Westminster in November 1841. The Lord Mayor was Sir John Pirie, a Plaisterer. The Prince's health was drunk from this bowl on board. The inscription was added in 1847. The Goldsmiths also have a long banner or streamer 30ft by 6ft. It bears the Company Arms, the Arms of John Garrett (Lord Mayor in 1824) and William Taylor (Lord Mayor in 1835), and St Dunstan. It is of silk and painted on both sides. Finally, the Company has a finial believed to be from the cabin of one of its barges. A carving of a wooden cup with cover is mentioned. It is just possible that this is the carving, which has been adapted for another purpose.

The Goldsmiths' Bargemaster's badge made by John Payne,
Goldsmith 1761

A figure of St Dunstan, patron saint of the Company

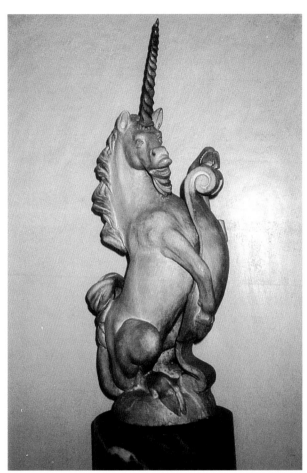

A unicorn, one of a pair, similar to those which decorated the Company barge

A maplewood wine bowl banded with silver which was used on the barge, made to commemorate the birth of Edward VII

A wooden finial believed to have been part of the decoration on the barge

*A carving of the arms of the Goldsmiths' Company which may
have been intended for the stern of their barge.*

THE SKINNERS' COMPANY (6 OR 7)

THE SKINNERS' COMPANY originated as a guild of furriers. They were engaged in the manufacture and sale of furs used mainly for trimming the garments of wealthy citizens. Edward III granted them their first Charter in 1327 which enabled them to hold land as well as to regulate their trade in the City. The Company no longer has control over their craft but still contributes towards a number of charities. It alternates in precedence with the Merchant Taylors' Company as the result of a judgement by Sir Robert Billesden (Mayor in 1484), in settlement of a dispute between the companies.

The Skinners' Coat of Arms, illustrated here by one of their banners, was granted in 1550 and depicts three ermine caps (the most esteemed furs in which skinners dealt), tasselled and enfiled with gold crowns supported by a lynx and a marten, the furs from which were much prized. The lynx also forms the crest. The motto is 'In Christo fratres' (Brothers in Christ).

As with other Companies, the Skinners hired a barge for the early processions on the Thames. On one occasion in 1518, when Thomas Mirfine, a Skinner and great grandfather of Oliver Cromwell, was Lord Mayor the Company had the use of Cardinal Wolsey's barge. There is a reference to hiring in 1540 when the Mayor and Commonalty of the City were commanded to wait upon the King and Queen (Henry VIII and Anne of Cleves) from London to Greenwich. The Skinners' first barge was built at a cost of £114 10s in 1656 when Sir Robert Tichborne was Lord Mayor. Sir Robert had the distinction of sitting at the trial of Charles I and was one of those who signed the warrant

for the King's execution. He was subsequently knighted by Cromwell. However when Charles II came to the throne in 1660 he was convicted for high treason. Times could be difficult even for a Lord Mayor.

In 1738 the Company decided to have a new barge. This barge was repainted for Sir Robert Kite, Skinner, when he was Lord Mayor in 1766. Besides the processions to Westminster, the Skinners' were present in a barge when the new London Bridge was opened by William IV in 1831. When in 1849 the Coal Exchange was opened on behalf of the Queen by Prince Albert, they attended the royal procession to the Custom House and back to Whitehall. Their last barge, built by Mr Hall, was sold in 1858 to Mr Searle and used by Queen's College, Oxford as a house boat. Details relating to the barge can be found in the Company's archives held at Skinners' Hall.

The Skinners' Bargemaster's Badge is dated 1719; the maker is not known. The Bargemaster's coat, which does not survive, was scarlet with a pleated skirt and ermine collar and cuffs. Six of the caps belonging to the crew have survived. They are of red velvet trimmed with ermine with the crest of the Company as a badge on the front. The crest is a leopard but on the cap it is not looking to the dexter as in the official Arms, which is unusual.

The Company is fortunate in having part of a long banner, which is exhibited in their Hall with two trumpet banners showing the Company Arms. There is also a small sketch part-tinted showing the Company barge by A. Nibbs. It is believed to have been painted in about 1839. The original was at one time in the Brighton Museum. The copy was made in c.1916.

A silk banner depicting the Skinners' Arms

One of two trumpet banners

Two sections of the Skinners' long banner

The Bargemaster's badge purchased in 1719.
The maker's mark has not been identified

One of four surviving caps belonging to the barge crew.
The badge is the crest of the Company

THE MERCHANT TAYLORS' COMPANY (6 OR 7)

THE MERCHANT TAYLORS' COMPANY was originally a religious and social fraternity which developed into a craft association of tailors and linen armourers. The latter made padded tunics to wear under armour. Their first Royal Charter was granted by Edward III in 1327. Their full name in a Charter of 1503 was The Guild of Merchant Taylors' of the Fraternity of St John the Baptist in the City of London.

The first Grant of Arms and crest was made in 1481. The present Arms, crest and supporters were granted in 1586, and depict a pavilion in imperial purple garnished with gold and lined with ermine, between two mantles also in imperial purple lined with ermine, and a lion, supported on either side by a camel which alludes to the Company's eastern trade. The crest depicts a lamb on a green mount surrounded by sunbeams; the motto is 'Concordia parvae res crescunt' (With harmony small things become great). The Company still has the full Arms from the stern of their last barge. The carving is over 7ft tall and is exhibited by the main staircase in their Hall.

The earliest entry in the Company accounts relating to barges shows expenses for hiring a barge on the accession of Henry VII and again in 1558 when Queen Mary was taken to the Tower on being proclaimed Queen. Hiring a barge for ceremonial occasions does not appear to have been very satisfactory and in 1640 the Company ordered their first barge to be built. Six barges were built for the Company between 1640 and 1800. There are references in the archives at Merchant Taylors' Hall to eight trumpet banners in 1457, a tilt or awning for a hired barge in 1640, and a new set of banners in 1764, the banners being The Arms of the Sovereign, the City, the Company, the figure of their patron saint St John the Baptist, the Company Crest and the Union. At the same time, rollers for the banners and cases for new figures were included. Unfortunately there are no details of the figures. There are excellent plans of the 1800 barge in the archives. This was built by Richard and Thomas Roberts for £1,607. It was 79ft overall and had 14ft beam. A scale model is exhibited at the foot of the staircase in the Hall. This was their last barge and was sold to Oxford University Boat Club in 1846 for £125. It survived until 1900, when it was finally broken up. A recent find has been of a photograph of the barge taken at Oxford (see page 152). The Company bargehouse was located at Lambeth.

The Bargemaster's Badge made by Whipham and Wright in 1764 is now attached to a large snuff box, forming the lid. A coat believed to have belonged to the Bargemaster has survived together with three peaked caps made of blue velvet belonging to the crew and three of their sleeve badges, showing the Company crest.

Model of the Merchant Taylors' Barge built by
Roberts of Lambeth, 1800. Length 79ft, beam 14ft

*A carving of the Merchant Taylors' Arms from the stern of their
barge. It is over 7ft high and exhibited in their Hall*

A badge worn by one of the Merchant Taylors' oarsmen

The Bargemaster's badge made by
Whipham and Wright in 1764

One of three surviving caps worn by the barge crew

The coat and trousers of the Bargemaster or coxwain

THE HABERDASHERS originated as a Fraternity whose patron saint was St Catherine of Alexandria. It most probably had its roots in a fraternity which worshipped at St Paul's Cathedral in 1389. Its members were haberdashers who sold ribbons, beads, purses, gloves, pins, caps and toys. They were joined by the Hatmakers and had the right to search all haberdashers' shops within three miles of the City. They received their first grant of Arms in 1446, an interpretation of which can still be seen borne by an Angel in their Hall. In 1448 Henry VI granted a Charter of Incorporation which entitled the Company to hold land.

The present Arms (not illustrated) date from 1503 which are a blue and white wavy field, representing the Haberdashers' ocean-wide commerce, with a lion symbolising their royal patronage, with the crest and supporters added in 1570. The crest depicts two naked arms issuing from clouds holding a laurel wreath. The supporters are on either side a goat of India flecked with red and membered gold. The motto is 'Serve and obey'.

The Company has a number of references to barges in its archives held at the Guildhall. One of the early accounts concerns Sir Stephen Peacoke, a Haberdasher who was Lord Mayor in 1532, when a barge was hired for his journey to Westminster. The Company escorted Anne Boleyn from Greenwich to Westminster to be crowned in 1533, when the barge was to be garnished with banners. In 1604 when Sir Thomas Lowe, a Haberdasher, was Lord Mayor, a barge is mentioned for the Company. On this occasion a silk coat and scarf were provided for the Bargemaster and Henry Wilde painted fifty-seven targets or small shields bearing heraldic devices to decorate the barge. It is said that one hundred and eighty chambers were discharged twice during the day, which would suggest that they had ample refreshment on board; however, it appears that this was actually the Haberdashers' returning salutes with their muskets. The Company had a large armoury for their trained band, part of the National Reserve Army raised by the Livery Companies. One of their muskets bearing the Company's Arms has survived and is exhibited in the Tudor Collection at the Museum of London. Other muskets of the same period are known to exist, including one in the Royal Collection at Windsor with the Arms of the Stationers' Company and another in the Royal Armoury with a powder horn bearing the Arms of the Goldsmiths' Company. In 1642 the Haberdashers made a large addition to their armoury by the purchase of 100 muskets and bandoliers.

In 1638 John Hall submitted an estimate of £320 to build a Company barge. There is an excellent description of this in the archives. It was to be of similar dimensions to the Fishmongers' and the Drapers' barges with eighteen oars. Carvings of the Company Arms with supporters on the stern, the patron saint St Catherine 4ft high, two sea nymphs 2ft 10in high, the King's Arms over the Master's seat and a figurehead which was not described, were all to be supplied with boxes to store the figures when not required afloat. The lute stern was to be carved and gilded. This barge was not built until 1656, and further barges were hired; for example in 1643 when John Fowke was a Sheriff, and in 1646 when Simon Edmonds was a Sheriff, the cost being £5 on each occasion. A new banner was purchased for £5 6s in 1640 to replace one showing Sir Nicholas Rainton's Arms, which had been 'spoyled on the water'. An embroidered barge cloth was purchased for £22 4s 2d for the new barge, and a bargehouse built at Lambeth for £4 per annum rent for forty-five years and a £20 fine. This seems to have been reduced to 10s by the Lord Archbishop of Canterbury in a document dated January 1692. In July 1747 John Cloves was appointed Bargemaster which was unusual in that he was already a Liveryman of the Company. There is no record that he was ever Master of the Company. He received the same salary as his predecessor. By 1754 the cost of maintaining the barge proved too expensive and it was sold to the Tallow Chandlers' for £262 10s. The same barge was later purchased by the Phoenix Assurance Company and on one occasion hired from them by the Clothworkers.

The Company still has the figure of St Catherine from its barge and the Bargemaster's badge dated 1689 is mounted on a snuff box (the maker is not recorded). The Company had a long barge banner or pennant, but unfortunately it was destroyed during the Second World War. A photograph remains and from this it has been possible to construct a replica. This shows the Union flag (as it was between 1707 and 1801), the Arms of the City with a fur hat, the crest of the City, the Arms of the Company and the crest of the Company. Between the compartments is the motto of the City – Domine Dirige Nos (God direct us).

A silver gilt badge of the Haberdashers' Bargemaster

St Catherine, patron saint of the Company

A carving of the original Haberdashers' Arms

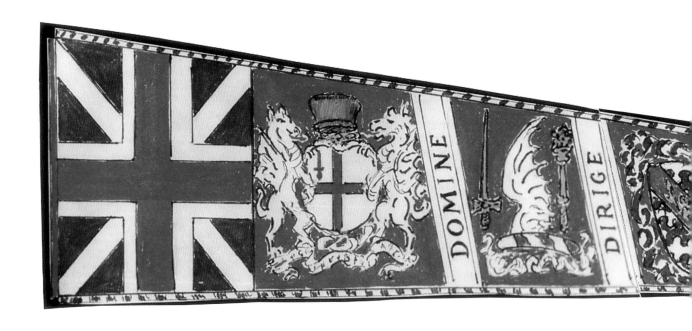

A reconstruction of the Company's long banner

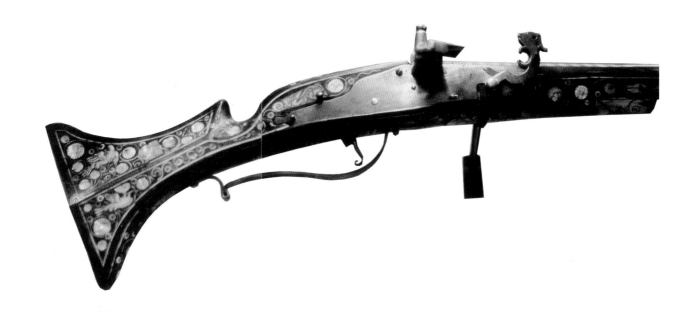

A musket c.1604, bearing the Haberdashers' Arms

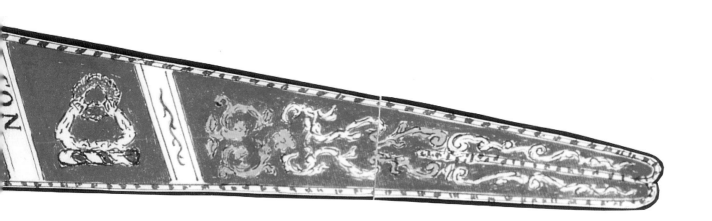

THE SALTERS' COMPANY (9)

THE SALTERS' COMPANY had its origin as a religious fraternity and its first licence as a guild was associated with the Church of All Hallows in Bread Street. The licence was granted by Richard II in 1394.

Further licences were received from Edward IV in 1467 and Henry VIII in 1510. Their Charter of Incorporation was granted by Elizabeth I in 1559. A Charter granted by James I in 1607 gave the Salters' Company powers of jurisdiction over all Freemen exercising the art of Salter in the City and for two miles beyond. Members of the Company not only dealt in salt, but were also drysalters and dealt in flax, hemp, logwood, cochineal, potash and chemical preparations. Arms were granted in 1530 and depict three covered salts garnished with gold, the salt shedding on both sides, supported on either side by an ounce (or lynx) with a crown around its neck and a chain. The crest is an arm issuing from water holding a salt as in the Arms. The motto is 'Sal sapit omnia' (Salt savours all).

Salt was a very important commodity used not only for cooking but for preserving, bleaching and tanning. England was unable to make sufficient salt for its needs and large quantities were imported from France. Some of this was unloaded at Queenhithe and some at Billingsgate, where it was used for preserving fish. The cost of salt apparently remained static for 250 years from 1270, when there was no inflation. On land, salt was transported for many years by pack horse, the normal load being two hundredweight.

There are not many references to processions on the Thames in the Company archives held at Salters' Hall, although since the Company had seventeen Lord Mayors between 1476 and 1801 and an additional eight Sheriffs who did not become Lord Mayor, it is likely that they took part quite often. The first reference is in 1591 when Sir William Webbe, a Salter, was Lord Mayor – the Company barge was ninth in the procession to Westminster. In 1662 the Company accompanied the King and Queen from Hampton Court to Whitehall, on which occasion flags depicting the Arms and two barge cloths were taken down from the Hall to use on the barge. Samuel Pepys and Lady Castlemaine watched the procession and a pageant from Whitehall Steps. In 1633 there is a record of a barge being hired for £4. In 1758 when Sir Richard Glyn, a Salter, was Lord Mayor, the Company borrowed the Brewers' barge and hired a bargemaster, his mate and eighteen oarsmen together with musicians, namely four French horns, four hautboys, two bassons and two trumpets.

The Company has one very large banner approximately 12ft by 6ft. This is painted on silk with a sleeve for a flag pole and is exhibited in their Hall. Eight shields or targets also have survived. These have been restored and have names on the back. They would have been carried in the procession on land and possibly hung over the sides of a barge on the water. One of these bears the name of John Adcock, Master in 1809, and another the name of Joseph Scott, Master in 1813. There is a record that the Company at one time possessed thirty shields and twenty-nine banners. Most of the latter would have been quite small and displayed on the roof of the bargehouse or cabin. In 1704, when Sir Owen Buckingham was Lord Mayor, a banner with the Arms of Queen Anne, the Standard of England, six pennants, twenty-four shields and two barge cloths, which were embroidered with the Company Arms, were used for a procession on the Thames.

*The large banner of the Salters' Company
which is exhibited in their Hall*

*The shield of Joseph Scott, Master in 1813,
showing the reverse with supports for carrying or
possibly hanging on the side of a barge*

The shield of John Adcock, Master in 1809

THE IRONMONGERS were originally known as Ferroners and were an effective body in 1300 when they took action against the smiths of the Weald over the quality of iron supplied for the wheels of carts in the City of London. By 1328 they were regarded as a firmly established brotherhood, joining in the elections of the City Officials and choosing four of their members to treat with the Mayor and Sheriffs. They received a Grant of Arms in 1455 and a Charter of Incorporation from Edward IV in 1463. The Company Arms embody various iron and steel objects (three gads and three swivels), with two lizards or salamanders as a crest, the legend being that salamanders were believed to be able to survive fire. Lizards as supporters were granted in 1923, although they had been used before then. The motto is variously 'God is our strength' or 'Assayer dure' (Try hard).

The Company had twenty-two Mayors or Lord Mayors and must have taken part in a number of processions on the Thames. The first record of hiring a barge was for travelling to Greenwich in 1533 to escort Anne Boleyn from Greenwich to the Tower on the occasion of her coronation, at a cost of 33s 4d. An additional 6d was paid for cushions. In May 1610 the Lord Mayor required the Company to meet Prince Henry at Chelsea and to accompany him by water to Westminster where he was to take his oath as Prince of Wales. In 1662 the Company attended Charles II and his Queen from Hampton Court to their Palace at Whitehall in the Company barge without their servants. At a meeting in North's Coffee House in 1685, members gathered to discuss arrangements for the Company to attend Lord Mayor's Day for Sir Robert Geffrye, an Ironmonger. Sir Robert was distinguished by being knighted by Charles II. The Company barge was to be used and four gallons of canary wine provided. The Admiral's Flag and the great streamer were to be taken, the Lord Mayor being Admiral of the Port of London and entitled to fly a white ensign defaced with the sword of St Paul. Five musicians and a man to 'play the tongues' were hired at a cost of £5. Ribbons were to be provided as necessary. The Company was to meet at the Grocers' Hall, move to the Guildhall and then march to Three Cranes Wharf, where they would take to the barge. After taking his oath at Westminster, the Lord Mayor was to return to Blackfriars Stairs, where the Royal Artillery Company would salute him with three volleys. The Artillery would be adorned in buff with shining headpieces, many of which were of massy silver. The Company would then process to Guildhall where the Lord Mayor might be entertained by a pageant. An inventory taken in 1707–8 lists the following for the barge: two large barge cloths; sixteen blue caps and coats for the watermen; the Company Arms, carved in wood and painted for the stern; a chest of flags, ensigns and sixteen blue cushions.

In 1719, when Sir George Thorold, an Ironmonger, was Lord Mayor, the barge was to be decorated with the King's Arms, the City and the Company Arms; the barge doors were to be painted with the figures of Peace, Plenty, Charity and Justice, and on the front of these doors a sea horse; on the panels on each side Neptune and Aphrodite were to be painted. Other decorations included flowers, fruit and shells and gilded lions, all of which were to be done by Mr Butler for £27. In 1740 a carver was hired to make a new shield for the stern of the barge and a figure of St Lawrence. In 1764 refreshments were to be supplied for the barge on Lord Mayor's day. No guests were to be admitted on board and no smoking was allowed. The Court also occasionally arranged excursions up river. In July 1768, a dinner was provided at the Swan at Chelsea for sixty persons.

The Company is known to have had its own barge in 1670, which was rebuilt by John Loftus in 1698. The carver was Joseph Robinson and the joiner John Bodle. The ornaments included mermaids, sea lions and an ostrich (which is alleged to have a cast-iron digestion and so be able to swallow iron). The carving of the ostrich is exhibited on the staircase in the Ironmongers' Hall. It has a horseshoe in its beak, which perhaps indicates part of the Company's trade, when horseshoes must have been in demand for the numerous horses used in the City. The carving of St Lawrence, patron saint of the Company, which would also have been carried on the barge on ceremonial occasions, is also shown on the staircase.

The Ironmongers had a bargehouse at Lambeth close to that of the Barbers. In 1763 the barge was replaced by a more resplendent one built by Mr Searle. The barge house or cabin had thirty-six plate-glass sashed windows. It was used for the funeral procession of Lord Nelson in 1806 and sold in 1809.

Among the treasures of the Company is a funeral pall of dark crimson on cloth of gold, with a border of black velvet, depicting the Company's Arms, the Virgin Mary and New Testament saints. It is dated 1515 and would have played an important part at the funerals of deceased members. There may even have been occasions when this was used on their barge.

The Bargemaster's badge of the Ironmongers' Company,
which forms the lid of a snuff box

The Ironmongers' Company flag painted on silk
and rather badly damaged

*A carving of the Company Arms. A similar carving would
have been used on the stern of their barge*

Part of a funeral pall dated 1515

*The figure of St Lawrence, patron saint,
carved by Joseph Robinson for the 1698 barge*

A carving of an ostrich made for the Company barge

THE VINTNERS' COMPANY was first recognised as a trade and social guild by a Charter of 1364 which granted them a monopoly of trade with Gascony and powers which included the right of search throughout England. They were incorporated in 1436 and received a licence in mortmain.

The Company controlled the wine trade in London and dominated it in the rest of the country during the Middle Ages. In 1553 Edward VI severely curtailed the country-wide right to sell wine. This, with the loss of the Chantries, led to a decline in the Company's importance and wealth. During the interregnum, when Parliament came to power, the Company suffered a penal tax on wine. The Great Fire destroyed their Hall in 1666 resulting in further great financial loss. In 1725 the Company lost the power of search and fewer members joined the Company. However, its estates grew in value and it was able to continue with its charities. Fortunately the right or privilege of selling wine without licence in the City and within three miles was retained. This right also applied to certain ports and thoroughfare towns between London and Dover and London and Berwick.

Arms were granted in 1447 which embody a chevron and three tuns. A crest and supporters were granted in 1957. The crest is a carvel laden with tuns, the mainsail of the carvel is charged with a cartwheel, the emblem of St Martin, the patron saint of the Company. The supporters on either side are swans (a cob and a pen) both nicked in the beak with the mark of the Company, with a riband around their necks from which hangs a bunch of grapes. These refer to the Company's right to own swans on the Thames. One of the early records of their interest in swans relates to when they cared for them during the great frost of 1522. The motto 'Vinum Exhilarat Animum' (Wine gladdens the heart) was registered in 1822.

The Company archives held at the Guildhall date from 1364. There are several references to taking part in pro-cessions on the Thames. In 1508 a barge was hired for 15*s* for the procession to Westminster on Lord Mayor's Day. It is likely that the Company also hired a barge in 1510 when they had two Sheriffs. In 1522 the Company took part in a procession on the Thames to welcome Emperor Charles V. It is further recorded that barges were hired in 1533 from John Sherborne for 28*s* 6*d.* for the coronation of Anne Boleyn, in 1540 to escort Anne of Cleves, and in 1612 for the Lord Mayor's procession to Westminster. By 1617 Peter Young was paid £6 per year to keep a barge ready for the Lord Mayor's procession, which fee also included the provision of oarsmen.

Soon after this the Company purchased a barge of its own and took out a twenty-one year lease on a bargehouse at Lambeth. In 1683, when Sir Henry Tulse, Grocer, was Lord Mayor, Samuel Dashwood was one of the Sheriffs. When he became Lord Mayor in 1702, the Vintners processed in their barge with the barges of the Grocers, Fishmongers, Goldsmiths, Mercers, Skinners and Weavers. In 1739 the Vintners obtained the lease of one of the Apothecaries' bargehouses at Chelsea. On some occasions, the Company may have embarked, on a hired barge or their own, from Three Cranes Wharf, close to the Vintners' Hall, where the Company used to unload wine from France. Until about 1775 the Vinters retained the service of a bargemaster and his mate.

There are four flags displayed in the Vintners' Hall bearing the City Arms, the Company Arms, the Arms of Frances Wyatt Truscott (Lord Mayor in 1879 and Master in 1880) and the Arms of E.K. Bailey who was one of the Sheriffs. These flags are believed to have been made in 1765, when B. Kennet was a Sheriff. They would have been used in processions on Lord Mayor's Day. At one time the Company had a White Ensign, believed to have been used during Swan Upping.

The Company still has its Bargemaster's Badge, hallmarked 1716, showing their patron saint St Martin dividing his cloak with a beggar. There is also a gorget, said to have belonged to the Bargemaster. This was made by Hester Bateman, a member of the Company, and dated 1789. It has small silver loops at the back as if it was at one time attached to material. If it was worn as a gorget, the Arms would appear to be upside down. An alternative position might have been on a hat. There is a seventeenth-century carving of St Martin and the Beggar, about the same size as the carvings of the patron saints of several other Companies which were carried on their barges in procession. However, there is no history of the figure of St Martin having been afloat. The Company also has an excellent painting of St Martin in the Court Room and it has recently com-missioned a painting depicting the Thames, their quay and their barge as it was in the past.

The Vintners' Swan Upping banner

*A carved figure of St Martin of Tours, patron saint of the
Vintners' Company and the beggar with whom he shared his cloak*

Part of the Vintners' funeral pall

The Bargemaster's badge, 1716

A piece of silver made by Hester Bateman dated 1789.
It is recorded as a gorget worn by the Bargemaster.
This seems unlikely as the Arms would be upside down

THE CLOTHWORKERS' COMPANY (12)

THE CLOTHWORKERS' COMPANY was formed by the amalgamation of the Fullers, incorporated in 1480, and the Shearmen, incorporated in 1508, both of which were originally branches of the Weavers' Company. The Clothworkers were incorporated by Royal Charter of Henry VIII in January 1528 as the Guild or Fraternity of the Assumption of the Blessed Virgin Mary of the Art or Mystery of Clothworkers. The Clothworkers' craft was the finishing of woven woollen cloth. The Fullers' task was to cleanse the cloth. To make it square and prevent it shrinking when drying, it was stretched on a hooked frame or tenter (often to the absolute limit under tension – whence the expression 'on tenterhooks') to obtain the maximum length and to remove creases. The cloth was scoured with the dried thistle-like heads of teasel plants to remove loose particles and raise the nap. The nap was sheared after stretching the cloth on a padded bench and securing it with double-ended hooks known as havettes or habicks. Both habicks and teasel appear on the Company Arms.

The Company Arms were granted in 1530 and the crest and supporters in 1587. The achievement was confirmed at the Visitation of the City in 1634. The Arms depict two habicks and a teasel, indicating the different activities of the Clothworker, with a ram standing on a green mount as the crest. The supporters are pelleted griffins; the motto is 'My trust is in God alone'.

The Clothworkers had twenty-four Lord Mayors between 1559 and 1850 and must have processed on the Thames on numerous occasions. The first reference in the Company archives (held at Clothworkers' Hall) to their hiring a barge is to escort Queen Anne Boleyn to the Tower in 1536, where she was to be judged. The next reference is not dated but must be between 1543 and 1548, when the Company went to Westminster in a chartered barge glorious with silken banners and streamers, with the Bargemaster in a hat bedecked with ribbons. Another early reference is when they shared a barge with the Skinners in 1576 to process to Westminster with the Lord Mayor. Hiring a barge was not always a success, sometimes two wherries were needed to carry the overflow. The Company decided to have the use of a barge built by William Forster to carry sixty men, to be ready at a day's notice. It was to have five pairs of oars. The charge was to be £5 to include the watermen's wages and food. No charge was to be made for the rushes for spreading on the deck. An embroidered barge cloth of azure woollen cloth was purchased. This barge appears to have been used for the first time in 1618.

The Company bargehouse was at Vauxhall, built on land shared with the Mercers and the Fishmongers.

A new barge was ordered in 1655. This was built by Alexander Saward at a cost of £115. A barge house was built for £120 and the barge cloth was enlarged. A Bargemaster, Anthony Earl, was appointed for no payment – except a free house and garden. This barge was used in 1657 to carry the body of General Blake and a few years later was used for the splendours of the Restoration. During the time of the Interregnum Alderman Sir John Ireton (Master 1652–3), brother of General Henry Ireton, was a Sheriff in 1651 and Lord Mayor in 1658. This may be the reason why the Clothworkers' barge was used for the funeral of General Blake. In 1662, with many other Livery barges, the barge was decorated with standards, streamers and other ornaments and used to escort Charles II and Catherine of Braganza to Whitehall. Sir John Robinson, Clothworker, was Lord Mayor. The procession was marshalled by the Water Bailiff. Anchors were used bow and stern to moor the barge, while awaiting Their Majesties' passage. There was also a pageant to which the Company had to contribute. Five trumpeters were engaged at a cost of £3.

William Hewer, Master in 1686–7, who was a friend of Samuel Pepys', is understood to have given the Company a new barge. In 1693 the Company barge was repaired. The Court of Assistants and their ladies were to have the use of it and to find some convenient place to dine. This was repeated in August 1695. The Assistants and their ladies were able to visit Putney and return to dine at Chelsea. In 1694 a fleet of Livery barges, gloriously bedecked, sailed to Westminster for the Lord Mayor, Sir Thomas Lane, Clothworker, to be presented. On their return they landed at Baynard's Castle for a procession on land and a pageant. A new barge was built at a cost of £230 in 1732 but was damaged by a lighter on Lord Mayor's Day fifty years later. Both lighters and Livery barges were difficult to navigate and it is therefore surprising that accidents do not seem to have happened more often. In the same year there was an order that the drinking of wine was to be limited on the barge. Eight other members of the Company became Lord Mayor during the next seventy years, when the barge must have been well used.

In 1799, the Company's last barge was no longer serviceable. When Sir John Perring Bt, Clothworker, was Lord Mayor in 1803 a barge was lent to the Company by the Phoenix Assurance Company. In 1850 when Sir John Musgrove, Clothworker, became Lord Mayor, the Company hired a barge for the last time and a shallop for the musicians. They did consider hiring a steamer but decided against it.

Very little, if anything, has survived from the barges. A carving of a Golden Ram, which might have been carried on the last Company barge, was destroyed by enemy action in 1941. However, a large flag or banner bearing the Company Arms survives at Clothworkers' Hall. It is very well painted on silk and approximately 12ft by 6ft. There is no evidence that this was ever carried on a barge, but a flag of similar design and size would have been at the stern of a Company barge on ceremonial occasions. The Company also has a carving of the Company Arms similar in style to a bow or quarter badge of other Companies.

The Clothworkers' Arms on a large banner of the type flown from the stern of a Livery Barge

*A carving of the Company Arms which may have been
a bow or quarter badge*

*The Bargemaster's badge, hallmarked 1787,
made by Henry Green, Clothworker*

A carved model of the Golden Ram from the Company barge destroyed by enemy action in the Second World War

The Clothworkers' Archery Mark, which at one time stood in Shepherd and Shepherdess Field near Islington

THE DYERS' COMPANY (13)

THE DYERS were first mentioned as a guild in 1188 by which time they had become very skilled in the art of producing colours from various natural materials such as the madder plant and kermes, an insect from which a red dye could be obtained. The Company was granted a Royal Charter of Incorporation by Henry VI in 1471. The Arms of the Company were authorised in 1577. They depict three bags of madder with a grain-tree as a crest, both of which represent two of the staple materials of the dyer's trade. The supporters are leopards (the badge of the House of Lancaster and Henry VI) spotted in colours, no doubt as tokens of the various colours the dyer could produce. The motto is 'Da Gloriam Deo' (Give Glory to God).

The Company does not appear to have had any Lord Mayors although Sheriffs elected in 1681, 1806, 1817, 1827 and 1835 were Dyers. The Company's main interest in the Thames is with the swans. They join with the Queen and the Vintners' Company in owning swans on the river.

They still take part in Swan Upping, having their own special mark to show which swans belong to the Company. The Company would have required a barge for Swan Upping but not one as large or difficult to handle as a Livery barge. It is possible that they might have used the same barge on ceremonial occasions for the Master and a small number of Liverymen. There is a reference in the Leathersellers' archives (held at the Guildhall) to the effect that they shared the Dyers' barge in 1682.

The Dyers have a silk flag 5ft by 10ft bearing the Company Arms, which is now under restoration at the Textile Conservation Centre at Hampton Court Palace. This may well have been used on a hired barge when various members of the Company were Sheriffs for the annual procession to Westminster, although there is no evidence of this. The Company also has a Bargemaster's Badge dated 1746 and hallmarked RC. This is still worn by the Bargemaster on ceremonial occasions.

The Dyers' Company banner which is receiving extensive restoration

The Dyers' Company's Bargemaster's coat and Swan Upping badge

Detail of the Dyers' Bargemaster's badge, 1746

THE BREWERS' COMPANY (14)

THE BREWERS became organised in 1292 when they sought redress for some of their grievances. By 1376 their Mystery was sending four of its members to represent their trade in Common Council. The Brewers' Company was incorporated under a Charter by Henry VI in 1437. They became quite a large and powerful Company; in 1469 their return to the muster for the City Watch was 210, the largest of all the companies and ten more than the Mercers. Their Charter conferred the right to acquire and hold land, to plead in court and to have four Wardens.

The first achievement of the Arms was approved in 1468 and was replaced by a grant in 1543. This embodied six barley sheaves and three kilderkins, with a demi-Moorish woman holding in either hand three barley ears as the crest. The motto is 'In God is all our trust'. The original Grant of Arms consisted of the Arms of the Company impaled with the Arms of the See of Canterbury and those of St Thomas à Becket, patron saint of the Company. The reason for the change in the Arms may be explained by the religious convulsions of the time; figures and devices relating to saints were removed from the Arms of several of the Livery Companies to cloak their religious origins. The Moorish maid in the Brewers' crest refers to the Saracen princess who rescued Becket's father Gilbert, when he was captured while on a pilgrimage to Jerusalem. They fell in love.

She eventually found her way to London, with very little knowledge of the language, and was reunited with Gilbert. After her conversion to Christianity they were married.

The Company had five Mayors, the first being Sir William Walderne in 1422. He translated from the Brewers' to the Mercers' Company in order to become Mayor. He was also the first recorded Mayor to travel to Westminster in a barge – the other Mayors being Sir Raphe Dodmer (or Dormer), who was sent to prison until he consented to translate to the Mercers' Company in order to become Lord Mayor in 1529; Sir John Parsons in 1703, who must have been one of the first to break the rule of the Great Twelve which continued until 1742; Sir William Calver in 1748; and Sir Crisp Gascoyne in 1752 (the first Lord Mayor to reside in the Mansion House). In addition eight members became Sheriffs. It seems likely that the Company must have processed on the Thames to Westminster on a number of occasions, either in its own barge or a hired one.

The Bargemaster's badge now forms the lid of a snuff box. It is hallmarked 1667 but the maker of the badge is not known.

The Brewers have one long banner or pennant, and two other banners, one with the City Arms and crest, the other with the Company Arms and crest. They also own a banner made to hang in the Guildhall in 1911. In addition to other treasures the Brewers' have an excellent funeral pall.

The Brewers' Bargemaster's badge, dated 1667

*A banner with the Brewers' Arms made to hang
in the Guildhall in 1911*

To M.r Joseph Dickinson Master of the Worshipfull Company of Brewers The Order of Procession.
For the Barges as Regulated by the R.t Hon.ble the Lord Mayor and Court of Aldermen
To be Observed on Monday the 10.th Day of November _____ 1766

1. Stationers			8. Iron Mongers		
2. Apothecary's	To Anchor		9. Merchant Taylors	To Anchor	
3. Tallow Chandlers			10. Goldsmiths		
4. Coopers	on		11. Fishmongers	on	
5. Brewers			12. Drapers		
6. Clothworkers	The Lambeth Side		13. Grocers	The Westminster Side	
7. Vintners			14. Skinners		

The City Barge to close the Procession.

It is Ordered _ That the said Barges be Rowed from the Three Cranes to Westminster In Procession _
As above Directed and to Return in the same Manner to Black Friars, Each Barge _
To Hold its Proper Rank and to keep an Equal Distance from Each Other So that the
Whole Procession be Formed in a Regular Line. _
It is further Ordered That the Rulers of the Watermen & Lightermen's Company do on that Day attend _
On the River of Thames to see the same Duly Performed And that a Copy of this Order _
be Delivered to Each of the Masters of the Severall Company's concerned _
Who are Desired to Conform to the Same _

Brewer's Barge to Precede the Clothworkers and to follow the Coopers. _

(Robert Glendoning) Clerk

*Two sections of the Brewers' long banner showing their crest,
the Moorish Maiden and their Arms.
The banner is unusual, being in the form of collage*

THE LEATHERSELLERS were granted certain rights by Edward III in 1372 for the treatment and sale of leather. Four years later they returned two members to Common Council. The Company had become prosperous and made a free gift of money to the King to support the French Wars. In 1444, Henry VI granted the Company a common seal, a licence in mortmain, and the power to hold assemblies and grant liveries. This would have included the right to search for bad or false wares. The Leathersellers have always maintained a close association with the companies that used leather in their trade. Six Companies, the Leathersellers', Cordwainers', Curriers', Saddlers', Glovers' and Girdlers' carried out searches together.

The Company received its first Grant of Arms in 1479. Supporters were added in 1505 and the Company's motto was first recorded in 1634 in a Confirmation of Arms by Sir Henry St George, Richmond Herald. The Arms embody three roebucks; the crest is a semi-roebuck; and the supporters are a roebuck and a ram. The motto is 'Sole Deo Honor et Gloria' (Honour and glory to God alone).

The first record in the Wardens' accounts for hiring a barge was on Lord Mayor's Day 1475, when Sir Robert Basset, Salter, processed to Westminster. The cost was 12s 4d for thirty-seven Liverymen. The next occasions recorded were in 1480 for 'the setting in of the Lady Margaret [of Anjou]' and in 1481 for the Lady Duchess of Burgundy, but no details of these occasions are given. In 1610 a barge was hired to escort Prince Henry from Chelsea to Westminster to be invested as Prince of Wales, at a cost of £3 16s.

Unfortunately, he died of typhus two years later. In the Court minutes of 1613, a barge was hired with new standards, streamers and other accoutrements; the minutes do not state the purpose. At about this time the Company sometimes shared a barge with the Haberdashers' Company.

Sir Thomas Andrew became Lord Mayor in April 1649, having been a Sheriff in 1642. The Court appear to have attended him to Westminster in a hired barge. James Bune was a Sheriff in 1643, but did not become Mayor. In 1662 the Company was present at a Pageant in celebration of the marriage of Charles II to Catherine of Braganza. The Company had a barge built by Mr Fortee for £30 in 1664. There are details of the Bargemaster's accounts in the Company archives, held at Leathersellers' Hall, which include the purchase of a barge cloth and embroidering of the same. Other details recorded include the occasion when some damage to the barge was inflicted by the barge of the Goldsmiths' Company. In 1684 the barge was quite worn out and the Company had to return to hiring one.

In 1806 the Company declined to take part in Lord Nelson's funeral procession on the Thames, as they had no barge. Thomas Smith became Lord Mayor in 1809, having been Sheriff in 1805, which may have been the occasion when they hired the old City barge and borrowed watermen's jackets from the Ironmongers' Company. Cockades of the Company colours – red and white – were worn.

Leathersellers' Hall was severely damaged by enemy action in 1941 and most of the contents destroyed. Nothing remains belonging to a barge, either owned or hired.

*The Leathersellers' tapestry depicting the
full Arms of the Company*

*A carpet showing the Arms of the Leathersellers, the Saddlers,
the Cordwainers and the Glovers; all were associated with each other*

THE PEWTERERS' COMPANY (16)

THE PEWTERERS were an organised body with powers sanctioned by the Mayor and Aldermen in 1348. They were incorporated in 1473 by a Charter granted by Edward IV, allowing the Company to regulate the standard of workmanship, the training of craftsmen and the wages and prices to be set. The charter also granted the guild the right to search throughout England. The Company's own records are extant from 1451 and are held at the Guildhall. The Company still acts today under the Charter granted by Queen Anne. For two hundred years from the Charter of Edward IV, pewter, an alloy predominantly of tin with small percentages of copper or lead being added as hardening agents, depending on the grade required, was by far the best material for plates, dishes and drinking vessels. The manufacture of pewter throughout England was monitored by the Company. By the end of the eighteenth century alternative materials gradually superseded pewter.

The first Company Arms included a representation of the Assumption, recalling the Company's origin as a Fraternity in honour of the Virgin Mary. During the Reformation the Company found it wise to eliminate religious symbolism and in 1533 new Arms were granted. In 1573 a crest, supporters and mantling were approved. The Arms depict three strakes (a symbol of the Pewterer's trade) and three roses on budded stalks, supported on either side by a sea horse with tail. The crest depicts two arms holding in both hands erect a pewter dish. The motto is 'In God is all my trust'.

It is recorded in the Company archives, held at Pewterers' Hall, that barges were hired on several occasions. The earliest mention is of a barge hired in 1451 for 5s, for a procession with Sheriffs to Westminster. The Lord Mayor was Sir William Gregory, Skinner; the Sheriffs Mathew Philip and Christopher Wharton. In 1480 a barge was hired with other costs for 12s when Lady Margaret, mother of Henry VII, went overseas. In 1530 the Company accompanied the Lord Mayor, Sir Thomas Pargitor, Salter, to Westminster when the cost of hiring the barge was 17s 4d with 8d for drinks for the crew. In 1532 the Pewterers hired a barge from the Duke of Norfolk for 22s to escort Queen Anne Boleyn from Greenwich to Westminster for her coronation. Other costs included 6s 4d for the Duke's

servants, 8s for the crew's breakfast, 2s for beer, 6d for bread and 2s for the crew. A barge with twelve oars was hired in 1538 for a similar procession to Westminster. In 1539 the Company hired a barge to escort Anne of Cleves from Greenwich at a cost of 20s. There is also a reference to the hiring of a barge for 20s, and the fitting of eleven targets or small shields for 15d and painting of streamers 16s 8d as decoration to a barge for a water pageant in the same year. In 1623 a barge with eight rowers and a barge cloth, to accommodate forty persons, was hired for the Lord Mayor's procession. In 1653 James Philips was a Sheriff and the Company may again have been represented in a hired barge. In 1661, twelve new banners for the barge cost £9.

In 1662 a new barge was ordered costing £181 5s 6d. Presumably this was used for the procession and pageant for Catherine of Braganza. On 23 June 1681 it was reported that the barge was not fit for further use and by 16 July 1686 the Company's second barge was ready for launching. The second barge was sold in 1699 for £8. Welch's *History of the Pewterers' Company* indicates that a third barge was subsequently built, although there appears to be no record of this. The salary of Mr Pike, the Bargemaster in March 1664, was fixed at £3 yearly. In 1670 the Bargemaster and sixteen oarsmen received £3 16s for Lord Mayor's Day. One of the watermen whose blue coat was lost was paid 5s for a new one. On 10 April 1717 it was ordered that the Companys' joint interest, with the Haberdashers' Company, in a bargehouse be let or disposed of and by 15 June the Master reported that it had been let to a waterman in Southwark for £5 per annum. In 1817 the Company had another Sheriff, George Alderson. There is no record of hiring a barge on this occasion.

At Pewterers' Hall there is a Bargemaster's badge in pewter and an excellent Coat of Arms which may well have been on a barge. It is about the correct size to have been on the cabin rather than on the stern of the vessel. The Pewterers have a large flag or banner 12ft by 6ft bearing the Company Arms as they were after the Reformation, that is without the figure of the Virgin Mary. It is painted on silk with a sleeve for the flag pole. They also have part of a funeral pall bearing their Arms which are beautifully embroidered. It is dated 1662 and is on display in the Company Hall.

*A carving of the Pewterers' Company Arms
probably from their barge*

*A window showing the Arms of the Pewterers
before the Reformation*

Part of the Pewterers' funeral pall, dated 1662

A flag with the Arms of the Pewterers' Company

The Pewterers' Bargemaster's badge

A carved shield, from the Company barge, dated 1672
with the initials of the Master, Thomas Gregg

THE FIRST REFERENCE to the Barbers conducting their own affairs was in 1308, when Richard le Barber was presented to the Court of Aldermen and ordered to search through the whole of his craft to ensure that there was no scandal or improper behaviour. Barbers were then accustomed to practising minor surgery; major surgery was undertaken by surgeons, most of whom had learnt their skills in the service of the Crown in various wars. Later the Company examined surgeons for the Navy, who had the responsibility of attending to all sick or wounded members of the ship to which they were posted.

The Barbers were granted their first Charter in 1462 by Edward IV. In 1511 an Act was passed requiring all those who practised medicine or surgery within London and a seven mile radius to be licensed, after examination, by the Bishop of London or the Dean of St Paul's. In 1540 there was a most important development when Henry VIII approved the union of the Barbers and Surgeons of London by statute, which gave the Company a monopoly of surgery in London and the suburbs and powers to suppress the fraudulent and unqualified. The Company still has a commemorative painting of the event by Hans Holbein. Earlier, Henry had presented the Company with a silver-gilt grace cup and a silver-gilt and enamel instrument case.

The Company was granted Arms in 1569 which embody fleams, double roses crowned on spatters, and on a cross a lion passant gardant. The fleams were razor-sharp instruments used in blood letting and the spatters are spatulas, blunt instruments for spreading ointment or holding down the tongue to examine the throat. The crest depicts Opinicus, a fictitious beast, part lion, part eagle and part camel which suggests the qualities needed in a surgeon, and the supporters are lynxes. The motto is 'De Praescientia Dei' (from the foreknowledge of God). The arms of the Company are represented on an oak shield, c.1664, over a doorway in the entrance hall, which was formerly on the prow of the Company's barge. Another, larger carving of the arms, also about 1664, from the stern of the barge is placed over a doorway nearby.

The Company's first Sheriff was Sir John Ayliffe in 1548. He translated to the Grocers' Company but did not become Lord Mayor. The second Sheriff was Sir John Frederick in 1655 who also translated to the Grocers' Company to become Lord Mayor in 1661. A barge was hired for his procession to Westminster at a cost of £4 11s. The next Lord Mayor from the Company was Sir Humphrey Edwin in 1697. He had been Sheriff in 1688 and translated to the Skinners' Company to become Lord Mayor. Other Sheriffs were appointed in 1674 (two), 1711, 1714 and 1718. None of these proceeded to become Lord Mayor.

It is possible that the Company was present at a procession on the Thames in 1540, when ten barges, richly hung with targets and banners, escorted Henry VIII on the occasion of his marriage to Anne of Cleves. The procession was saluted by above a thousand chambers (rounds) of ordnance by the Tower of London and by ships as they passed. In 1622 the Court ordered a seven- or eight-oared barge to hold all the Livery for Lord Mayor's Day from Jones the Waterman at a cost of £4. In 1662 a barge was built by Henry fforty for £115. Other costs were £4 10s for twenty suits and caps for the crew, £29 10s for flags by Mr Blackmore the Herald Painter, a carved Opinicus for the bow of the barge, £11 for a barge cloth from Mr Rolls plus £15 for embroidering it, and £35 to Mr Good for painting the barge. There are details of the lease of land at Lambeth from the Archbishop of Canterbury to build a bargehouse for which the Archbishop's servants were paid just over £10 in gold. The bargehouse was built at a cost of £214 and was later shared by the Drapers and the Ironmongers until 1723 when the lease was not renewed; the barge itself had been disposed of in 1698.

The Company has a Bargemaster's badge of silver dated 1735 and made by Robert Lucas. There are also two sleeve badges made of base metal and painted with the Company arms, though these are rather larger than those usually worn by barge crew. A banner showing the full arms which is painted on silk and is approximately 4ft by 6ft was the gift of Past Master Sidney Young in 1885, as no banner associated with the barge had survived.

The Barbers' banner with full Arms painted on silk, 1885

The silver Bargemaster's badge made by Robert Lucas in 1735

The Barbers' Company bow badge

The Barbers' Arms from the stern of their barge

THE CUTLERS' COMPANY (18)

THE GUILD OF CUTLERS is known to have had a Hall in 1285. The first Articles were sanctioned by the Lord Mayor in 1344 and Ordinances were made in 1370. The Articles gave the power of search and the right to oversee the cutlery trade. Henry V granted the first Charter to the Company in 1416 in the year following the Battle of Agincourt. The Charter gave the right to hold property and created the offices of Master, two Wardens and a Court of Assistants.

The Company was granted Arms in May 1476 which depict three pairs of swords with hilts and pommels in gold. The crest was granted in 1622 and depicts an elephant armed and harnessed in gold bearing on its back a castle upon which two pennons are displayed. The supporters are two elephants. The elephant is presumed to allude to the ivory employed for the hafts of products. The motto was originally 'Pervenir a bonne foy' which later became 'Pour Parvenir a bonne foy' (To succeed through good faith.).

During the period under review, the Company had three Lord Mayors – William Bridgen in 1763, Henry Winchester in 1834 and Robert Walter Carden in 1857. There was one Sheriff who did not become Lord Mayor, Sir R. Hopkins in 1723. The Company hired a barge on a number of occasions. The first reference was in 1442 to Westminster at a cost of 4s. This may have been to accompany the Lord Mayor who was an Ironmonger; neither of the Sheriffs were Cutlers. The next reference was to join a procession for Edward IV in 1462. In 1465 a barge was hired for the Coronation of the Queen at Westminster, the cost being 6s 2d. In 1470 a barge was hired for 8s 4d when Edward IV came to London by water, and the bargemen received 20d for their dinner. In 1480 a barge was hired to accompany Lady Margaret, mother of Henry VII, for 14s 8d. The Company processed by barge to accompany Anne Boleyn from Greenwich to Westminster in 1533 for her coronation and in 1603 banners were purchased to accompany the coronation procession of James I of England and VI of Scotland.

In October 1616 the Company processed from Richmond to Westminster on the occasion of the appointment of Charles as Prince of Wales. There were over thirty barges present on this occasion. They were instructed to proceed in an orderly fashion – 40ft between barges, in two columns 80ft apart. In 1662 a barge was hired for 40 Liverymen, with a fair cloth and decorated with banners and streamers, to escort Charles II and Catherine of Braganza. In 1763, when the first Cutler Lord Mayor William Brigden processed to Westminster on the Thames, the Company used the Ironmongers' barge. Music was provided by two kettle drums and two trumpets. The refreshments were cakes and wine. By permission of the Queen, an elephant processed with them on land.

The Company still has a great streamer which was used on a barge in the procession of 1763. On land it was carried with poles by four bearers wearing cockades. The streamer, or pennant, is over 30ft long and is now exhibited in the Cutlers' Hall high up behind the Master's chair. Parts of it are very dark and difficult to see. From the staff end it shows in sections the Cutlers' Arms, Britannia, the City Arms and a Roman fasces with the rod of Mercury. Ten shields or targets are exhibited in the Cutlers' Hall. In the Lord Mayor's Procession in 1834, when Alderman Henry Winchester was Lord Mayor, pensioners carried these and three others for members of the Court. A barge was hired, on this occasion, with sixteen bargemen. The Company embarked at Southwark Bridge and thence by water to Westminster returning to Blackfriars Bridge. The Beadle is said to have stood in the bow – usually this was the position of the Bargemaster; perhaps he was acting for him. In 1835, the same Lord Mayor accompanied the King to Greenwich in a barge. On this occasion there were only four barges: those of the Mercers, the Goldsmiths, the Cutlers and the Stationers.

It was Sir Robert Walter Carden, Cutler, who finally stopped the Lord Mayor's processions on the Thames when he became Lord Mayor in 1856. There appear to be several reasons for this. One was the cost which was quite heavy. Another was the great increase in merchant traffic, making navigation difficult; a large procession would have interfered with trade. At the same time the City lost the management of the port and the river to the Thames Conservancy. The roads had improved, making a procession on land much easier. Lastly, the number of steam boats was increasing and they travelled much faster than sail or rowing boats. Livery barges were not easy to navigate, especially in a strong tide and wind.

A flag bearing the Arms of the Cutlers' Company

*Two sections of the Cutlers' long pennant showing a Roman
fasces with the rod of Mercury and a figure of Britannia, 1763*

A portrait of Sir Robert Carden, the Lord Mayor who stopped the river processions in 1857

The Arms of the Commonwealth with the escutcheon of Oliver Cromwell, used instead of the Royal Arms when Cromwell was Lord Protector

Shields of the Company and two of the Masters. These have handles for use in procession on land or water

THE BAKERS' COMPANY (19)

THE FIRST KNOWN records of the existence of the Bakers' Guild are contained in the great Pipe Rolls of Henry II which listed the yearly 'farm' of one gold mark paid by the Bakers from 1155 onwards. Only the Weavers' Guild has an entry a few years earlier. The farm was a form of tax on bread and it had the advantage of absolving them from further tolls which were customary in markets and fairs. As the producers of one of the most important of foods, especially for the poor, bakers were strictly controlled. The Bakers had the responsibility of enforcing these laws within the City and for a radius of two miles. They had the legal powers to hold a Court and to punish short weight and other offences. To avoid giving short measure an extra piece of bread was given with each loaf or an extra loaf with twelve loaves (hence the bakers' dozen). The Bakers still have a low balustrade or bar across their Court Room, at which offenders had to appear. The Assize of Bread ended in 1815 and the Company was relieved of its responsibility of controlling the trade.

At first there was just one Bakers' Company. It later divided into the White and the Brown Bakers. The White Bakers received their first recorded Charter from Henry VII in 1486. The Brown Bakers obtained a separate Coat of Arms in 1572, a Charter in 1614 and were incorporated in 1621. They separated from the White Bakers in 1622 but settled their differences and rejoined to make one Company in 1645.

A record of the first Arms of the Bakers was found in an ancient stained-glass window from the Church of St Andrew Undershaft dating back to 1461 before the foundation of the College of Arms in 1484. The present Arms were granted in 1536 and depict three gold garbs on a barry wavy of six with two gold anchors and an arm issuing from a cloud radiated holding a gold balance. The garbs or sheaves are the source of the bakers' products and the balance in divine hands represents the fair dealing through the agency of the Assize of Bread. The anchor is the emblem of St Clement, Patron Saint of the Company and third Pope, who was sentenced to drowning with an anchor round his neck by the Romans, for preaching Christianity. These Arms were followed by a crest and supporters in 1590. The crest depicts two arms issuing out of a cloud holding in their hands a chaplet of wheat; the supporters are on either side a buck, gorged with a chaplet of wheat. The two bucks are an allusion to the use in the past of buckwheat. The Brown Bakers originally had one anchor and the White Bakers a similar shield but with two anchors placed vertically in chief. The motto is 'Praise God for all'.

The Bakers do not appear to have had any Sheriffs or Lord Mayors before the processions on the Thames ceased in 1856 but there is a record of hiring a barge in 1355, and again in 1485 when the cost was 8s 4d for the Lord Mayor's procession to Westminster. The Bargemaster's badge which was lost for a number of years, was found in a dealer's shop in Bristol and sold back to the Company early this century. The Company has four fenders which are embroidered with the Arms of the Brown Bakers, that is with only one anchor in chief. These would have been hung over the side of the barge as decorations on ceremonial occasions. There is an interesting mural in the Hall which shows a barge with six of the oarsmen and shields on the side of the boat. The shields bear the Arms of the Brown Bakers. The ancient Arms of the White Bakers included a triple crown representing the Blessed Virgin. It must have been deemed wise to remove this at the time of the Reformation.

A fender with the Brown Bakers' Arms

The Bargemaster's badge

The carved Arms of the White Bakers

A mural of the Bakers' barge decorated with shields

THE WAX CHANDLERS' COMPANY (20)

THE FIRST REFERENCE to the Guild of Wax Chandlers appears to be in 1330, when the Wax Chandlers was one of twenty crafts invited to contribute towards a present to Edward III. They gave 40s towards a total of 1000 marks. In 1364 the craft was ordered to elect masters to present to the Mayor to be sworn to oversee their fellow craftsmen. There were to be penalties for not making good wax and for poor wicks.

Torches or tapers of wax were needed for important ceremonies including funerals. One honourary task was to maintain a taper candelabrum at St Paul's. An important part of the street lighting was a lantern outside each house and a tub of water as a fire precaution. By 1484 the Company had become sufficiently prosperous to obtain their first Charter, which is still in their possession. Their grant of Arms followed in 1485. The Arms depict three gold morters royal and three red roses with gold seeds. The crest is of a maiden vested in a surcoat of cloth of gold and furred with ermine, kneeling amongst flowers and making a garland thereof. Unicorns gorged with a garland of flowers and with their horns wreathed in gold and red, were added as supporters in 1530. The motto is 'Truth is the light'.

There is no history of the Wax Chandlers' owning their own barge although the matter was discussed in 1664, but nothing came of it. It is likely that the Company hired a barge when they had a Lord Mayor or Sheriff for the procession to Westminster. There is a record of hiring a barge in the Company accounts of 1530 – 'to Westminster when the Lord Mayor made his oath, 30s 4d and wages of watermen and drinks to them', and also to go Swan Upping at a cost of 5s 1d. Again in 1532–4 – 'hire of barge for two years 22s, rushes for barge 8d and watermen 16d', both items for two years. These expenses included the great procession by barge for the coronation of Queen Anne in 1533. In 1532 the cost of hiring the barge for the Swan Upping had risen to 5s 10d. On these occasions the barge would have departed from Three Cranes Stairs. A barge was hired in 1664 for thirty Liverymen for £6 10s; and in 1691 for £4, with 5s 10d for 14 yards of blue and yellow ribbon (the Company colours) for the bargemen. A blue barge cloth is mentioned in an inventory in 1659 as being kept at the Hall. New banners are mentioned in 1714 including the King's banner, the City, the Company Arms and a streamer five yards long to be painted by Charles Wiseman. New banners were ordered for Alderman Cowan in 1831 when he was elected Sheriff. These were to be in the best style and cost 60 guineas. When he became Lord Mayor in 1837, he embarked at London Bridge for his procession to Westminster. Later in the day he entertained the Queen at Guildhall.

The Company has a flag or banner with the full Company Arms painted on silk, and a flag pole. This was made in 1911 to be hung in the Guildhall. It is approximately 4ft by 6ft and would be similar to one used on a hired barge on ceremonial occasions. The silver head of the Beadle's staff may have been part of the Bargemaster's badge. There were at one time two similar badges which may have been joined together.

The Wax Chandlers' Bargemaster's badge
attached to the Beadle's staff

The Wax Chandlers' Arms on a flag made for
the Guildhall in 1911

THE GUILD OF TALLOW CHANDLERS was originally formed in about 1300 as a religious fraternity in honour of Our Lady and St John the Baptist. In 1422 it received Letters Patent from Henry VI granting it powers to search and destroy all bad and adulterated oils. In 1462 the Tallow Chandlers were incorporated by Edward IV granting them a livery. By 1469 they were strong enough to supply the City Watch with sixty men. Although the guild was originally concerned with candle-making using animal fats (as opposed to beeswax which the Wax Chandlers used) they also acquired some control of the trade in other products. In 1557 the Company was empowered to search for, weigh and measure all soap, vinegar, barrelled butter, salt, oils and hops within the City and suburbs. It also dealt in an assortment of domestic goods such as mustard, oatmeal, fine salt, packthread, brooms, pots and pans. It too was involved in street lighting in 1573 when the law required every house to show a light at the front door. However, the introduction of oil lighting and the granting of monopoly patents to street lighting contractors towards the end of the seventeenth century was a partial cause of the decline of the Company's prosperity and the use of its powers. The Company has occupied the same site since 1476 and retains a close link with heating and lighting through BP, British Gas and the edible oil industry.

A Grant of Arms was made in 1456. The Arms depict three doves each holding in its beak a gold olive branch with the head of St John the Baptist in a charger radiated as the crest. The supporters were added in 1662 and are on either side an angel vested, winged and crowned with gold stars. Both the crest and the doves symbolise St John the Baptist. The motto is 'Ecce agnus Dei qui tollit peccata mundi' (Behold the lamb of God that taketh away the sins of the world).

There are over 140 references to a barge in the Company archives, held at the Guildhall, from 1557 to 1799 when the Company's barge was sold for £50. The first mention is in 1557 when one was hired at a cost of 20s and 'a cord for the Bargemen 2d'. In 1558, 16s was paid to the Bargeman to wait on the Queen's grace for the Company when Her Grace Queen Elizabeth came from Westminster to the Tower of London. In 1573 a barge cloth was hired for 16d. Again in 1611 a barge was hired from Walter Shellings with a broad cloth, rushes and boards to convey the Livery every Lord Mayor's Day for 44s. By 1649 the cost had risen to £4 6d apiece for ten men for their breakfast. In 1662 the Company hired a handsome barge, for £5, well fitted to carry the Company to attend His Majesty Charles II and Queen Catherine from Hampton Court to Whitehall, on which occasion no person of the Livery was to bring his son or servant.

In 1666 the Tallow Chandlers shared the Goldsmiths' barge to Westminster, Sir Joseph Sheldon, a Liveryman, being one of the Sheriffs. Sir Joseph translated from the Tallow Chandlers to the Drapers' Company to become Lord Mayor in 1675. Sir Joseph 'out of his great affection to the Company freely provided a barge for the Company, when and as often as they should attend Lord Mayor's Day or otherwise and that a bargehouse be hired to prevent it from damage'. He also provided a barge cloth. The barge would have required sixteen able Watermen to row, provided by Walter Snelling, who was appointed steersman to the Company in 1611. His duties appear to have been those of a bargemaster. The wages for himself and the crew and for their breakfast amounted to £3 12s 6d.

In 1675 the Company and the Weavers both had a bargehouse on the Apothecaries' property at Chelsea. The Court Minutes refer to '...lease dated 20 September 1675 to the Weavers Company of a piece of ground there for £50 years and a half and eleven weeks from Lady Day 1675 at £140 Free and 30s per annum whereon is built two Barge houses one belonging to the Company...and the other to the Weavers...' Mr Thomas Gammon, carpenter, was paid £270 for building this double bargehouse of which cost the Weavers paid half.

In the Court minutes of 1669 there is an unusual entry – 'Paid for a Road Stone and chain for the barge £3 15s'. There must have been times when it was very necessary to anchor. In 1691 it was ordered that 'the Wardens do cause the Roadstone [road stone] belonging to the barge to be made more useful either by adding to it, or otherwise as in their discretions shall seem meet'. In other words the anchor dragged. A further stone and more chain were added. The type of anchor is surprising and must date back to Biblical times and beyond. It would resemble one of the four anchors cast out astern when St Paul's ship was in danger of being wrecked and those onboard prayed for the morning.

There is a very full description of a barge to be built for the Company in 1694. It was to be 70ft long, the house or cabin 30ft and the work to be finished as well as that recently built for the Fishmongers. This account includes oak stairs to the rear of the barge cabin, a carving of the Arms for the stern, two lions and a turtle dove, also new flag poles. The cost was to be £120 not including the carving and gilding. Mr Samuel Audney was to be employed for the carving and Mr Thomas Parkins for the painting and gilding. The Company's old barge was sold for £6. In 1695 the Company's Bargemaster, Mr Henry Batten, received a new coat and breeches at a cost of £2 13s 8d. Again in 1754 they sold their barge, except for the shields, carved works and wainscot forms and the following year purchased the Haberdashers' barge for £268 19s 9d.

In 1777 the Company agreed to the Coopers' Company using their barge for ten guineas and all other expenses. This was when Sir James Esdaile, Cooper, was Lord Mayor. In 1786 the Tallow Chandlers' purchased from the Goldsmiths' Company an iron ornament for their own barge. The barge was finally sold in 1799 for £50 to the Phoenix Assurance Company.

It appears that the Bargemaster's badge was not returned by his widow in 1785 and that a new one, costing not more than £6, had to be made. The Company still has this displayed in Tallow Chandlers' Hall together with a flag or banner showing their full Arms painted on silk complete with flag pole. It is approximately 6ft by 4ft and was presented to the Corporation of London to be hung in the Guildhall Library in 1911.

The Tallow Chandlers' Arms on a flag made for the Guildhall

The Tallow Chandlers' Bargemaster's badge, 1785

The Company's Arms on a bow badge

The type of stone anchor or roadstone,
mentioned in the Tallow Chandlers' Court minutes

The bar in the Tallow Chandlers' Court Room
at which offenders were tried

THE ARMOURERS' AND BRAZIERS' COMPANY (22)

THE ARMOURERS' AND THE BRAZIERS' existed as separate Companies in the late Middle Ages, but the Braziers' Company disappears from records in the early sixteenth century. The earliest Ordinances drawn up by the Armourers with the assent of the Corporation are dated 1322. Supervisors of the craft were appointed and had the power of search to approve the quality of goods made. The Company received its first Charter from Henry VI in May 1453. Until the Reformation the guild provided a chaplain to celebrate divine service in the Chapel of St George in St Paul's Cathedral and all members attended a service there on the Day of their Patron Saint, St George. On ceremonial occasions members were frequently requested to provide an armed guard, especially on Lord Mayor's Day. When the use of armour for infantry and for cavalry (and their horses) was common, armoury must have been a thriving industry, but with the rapid decline in the wearing of armour after the Civil War the braziers, who were responsible for non-military metalwork, became more important. Many braziers came under the aegis of the Armourers Company and by the seventeenth century were an important part of it. In 1708 the Armourers' changed the name of their Company by Letters Patent to the present 'Armourers and Braziers'. The inclusion of the Braziers was probably also influenced by the extension of their industry to include copper and brass work.

The Company uses Arms by custom, there being no formal grant, and comprises the Arms of the Armourers, granted in 1556, impaling arms representing the Braziers'. The arms depict a tourney gauntlet (used for a type of tournament) between two pairs of swords, with a plate with a red cross between two helmets garnished. Arms representing the Braziers show three red roses on a gold chevron between two ewers and a three-legged pot with two handles. The crest is a demi-man of arms armed holding a mace of war in his hand. The supporters are two men in complete armour. The motto is 'Make all sure. We are one.'

Simon Wynchecombe was Sheriff in 1383–4 and Henry Rede in 1417–18. The Company took part in a number of ceremonial processions on the Thames. On New Year's Day 1537, the Company went by boat to Greenwich with their banners, targettes (shields) and 'George, standing over the rails' – 'George' being a figure of their patron saint wearing real miniature armour. The occasion was the visit of Henry VIII and Anne of Cleves to the Palace. The barges rowed up and down while the royal couple made their visit, perhaps because there was an ebb tide and the crew did not wish to have their craft stranded. Also there may have been a problem with finding a safe place to anchor, their anchors only being suitable for up-river conditions. The Company had a barge built in 1658 for £54, and 20s a year was paid for its berthing. In 1685 new streamers, caps of armour and coats suitable for the Watermen were ordered. The Court minutes of October 1772 record that 'The cap usually worn by the Bargemaster be repaired, cleaned and mended. If this cannot be done, a new one be provided.' Further mention is made of clothing in 1751 when instructions were given that on Lord Mayor's Day 'no man shall attend this Company in Black Armour... or wear the Brass Hatt or the Brass Coat of Mail'. The reason for this instruction is not clear. Perhaps it was considered dangerous afloat in case anyone should fall overboard. In November 1778, William Varney 'desired the favour of the Company to accept a new brass Cap proper to be worn on public days by the Bargemaster as a small mark of his esteem'. An undated reference to the Company meeting at the Green Dragon on Lambeth Hill states before 'taking to the water to attend his Majestie in his passage from Hampton Court to Whitehall'. Cold meat was to be provided and music to be arranged 'by the Wardens at their discretion and ribbons to be given to whome they think fit'. Livery barges were often saluted on ceremonial occasions from the shore, particularly when passing the Tower of London. The only indication of a barge being able to return the honour with cannon is the Company's possession of seven saluting guns. There is a carving of St George, made entirely of wood, in their Hall.

*A wooden carving of St George, the patron saint of
the Armourers' Company, wearing real armour.
This was carried on their barge*

A quarter badge of the Armourers, showing St George and the dragon

A second quarter badge with the Company Arms

A large brass ewer used for ale or rum on the barge with four of the seven saluting guns

THE GIRDLERS' COMPANY (23)

THE GIRDLERS received their first Letters Patent from Edward III in 1327 in which regulations of their craft were approved and they were authorised to elect one or two persons to overlook the rest to prevent defective or dishonest work. Before pockets were invented girdles were a most important article of apparel. Almost anything to be carried could be attached to the girdle, such as money in a pouch, keys, inkhorns, and even small books could be suspended from it. For weapons of various types a girdle or belt is still a first choice. For the more important citizens the girdle could be a work of art and of considerable value.

By 1376 the Company was entitled to be represented by four members on Common Council. Its first Charter was from Henry VI in 1448. The Company was joined by the Wireworkers and Pinners in a Charter from Elizabeth I. Unfortunately almost all the Company archives up to 1666 have been lost. The Company has had a connection with the Church of St Lawrence Old Jewry and at one time, before being incorporated, it was known as the Brotherhood of St Lawrence. St Lawrence was adopted as their Patron Saint. He was martyred for giving ecclesiastical treasure to the poor and was condemned to death by roasting on a gridiron in AD 258. The gridiron is his emblem and occurs in the Arms of the Company which were granted in 1454. St Lawrence also appears in the crest holding in one hand a gridiron and in the other a book

The Company had three Sheriffs – Richard Chambers in 1644, Stephen Eastwicke in 1652 and Thomas Sidney MP in 1844, who became Lord Mayor in 1853. Although they must have taken part in a number of processions on the Thames there are very few references to these in the archives, held at the Guildhall. There is a history of hiring a barge in 1650 for forty persons at a cost of £4 5s with £1 10s for trumpets and 6s for drums and fifes. This was during the Interregnum when processions appear to have continued. In 1662 a barge was hired with banners, which must have been to attend the reception of Catherine of Braganza. In 1735 two silk banners embroidered with silk and gold thread were purchased.

One large banner approximately 6ft by 12ft has survived and depicts the full Company Arms painted on silk with a red sleeve for a flag pole. It has a fringe of the Company colours, blue and white. It is probably mid-nineteenth-century and could have been used at the stern of a barge.

A large banner bearing the Arms of the Girdlers' Company

THE BUTCHERS' COMPANY (24)

THERE IS A TRADITION that there were divers slaughterhouses and a Butchers' Hall, where the craftsmen met, situated outside the City walls in Farringdon in AD 975. In 1180 the Butchers' Guild was fined for acting as a guild without a Charter or Licence, although a licence was granted by Henry II some time before 1189. In 1266 there is a reference to the Butchers' Guild punishing offenders showing and selling diseased meat. By 1331 the Butchers had gained control of the meat trade within the City – butchers had to submit to a price control of their meat, regulations regarding the disposal of offal and were not allowed to kill more than 300 oxen per week. In 1605 the Company was granted a Charter of Incorporation giving them control of the trade within the City and a radius of one mile.

The Butchers hired a barge in 1544 and in 1673. Although the records are not complete, the probability is that in both years this was for the Lord Mayor's procession to Westminster. The Company had three Sheriffs – William Mellish in 1798 when the Grocers accommodated the Butchers' Court on their barge to Westminster, James Alexander in 1802 and Thomas Challis in 1846, when a barge was hired and banners purchased at a total cost of £36 6s. It appears that on this occasion they shared the barge with another Company, possibly the Spectacle Makers who provided the Lord Mayor, or more likely the Carpenters who had the other Sheriff. Thomas Challis became Lord Mayor in 1852 when a barge was hired. In 1890 the Company hired the old City barge *Maria Wood* for a Court outing. Unfortunately the account lacks any details.

The Company Hall was severely damaged by a bomb in 1915 and almost demolished by a flying bomb in 1944. As a result, very little remains of their early possessions. However, there is a carving of the Company Arms that is the right size and appearance to have been attached to the cabin of a hired barge. The Company also has a flag or banner bearing its Arms, painted on silk and approximately 4ft by 6ft with a flag sleeve and pole. This was made for the Guildhall in 1911. The banner is to be restored and exhibited in the rebuilt Company Hall.

The Arms were granted by the College of Heralds in 1540, the motto being 'Omnia subjecisti sub Pedibus Oves et Boves' (Thou hast put all things under his feet, all Sheep and Oxen). The heraldic emblems represented in the armorial bearings relate to the Butchers' craft. The Arms depict two poleaxes, two bulls' heads and a boar's head between two bunches of holly. The winged bull which features in the crest is an allusion to St Luke, the Patron Saint of the Butchers. (St Luke's Day, 18 October was fixed as the day of the annual election day of the Mystery. On this occasion the Company processed suitably robed to the Church of St Bartholomew the Great for a service and to make their offerings, returning afterwards to their Hall to dine.)

*A carving of the Butchers' Arms, which may have
been on the cabin of a barge*

The Butchers' Arms on a flag made for the Guildhall

THE SADDLERS are known to have existed as a Brotherhood or Fraternity established in the vicinity of St Martin le Grand in the mid twelfth century. Here they had a close relationship with the canons and monks. The Saddlers' Guild was the first documented company; an agreement of *c.*1150 between the Saddlers' and the Canons of St Martin le Grand is held at Westminster Abbey. The importance of their craft was recognised in 1272 when two honest and discreet men were to be chosen to survey the craft in every city, town or borough where the craft was practised. It is thought that this may have been when a charter was granted but there is no firm proof. The first recorded Charter was granted in 1363, the first surviving Ordinances are 1364 and there is a Charter of Incorporation from March 1395. Arms were granted in October 1585 and depict a gold chevron between three saddles supported on either side by a horse, hoofed and bridled, with a plume of three feathers on its head. The horse also features in the crest, bridled and saddled. The motto is Hold fast, sit sure. Our trust is in God'.

The Company still has archives dating back to 1424 which are held at the Hall and which have a number of references to their barges. In 1609 a barge was hired for forty persons, presumably for the Lord Mayor's procession to Westminster. By 1662 the Company had its own barge and was looking for a convenient bargehouse and it therefore seems likely that they took part in the procession for Charles II and Catherine of Braganza. A barge cloth was listed in 1666. In 1670 Francis Dashwood gave £100 to buy banners, streamers and a barge cloth of crimson worsted in grain and crewel work. The cloth was embroidered with the Company Arms and other ornaments and had a ten-inch-wide border. It is interesting to note that crimson was the colour usually used on Royal occasions and that at most other times a blue cloth was used. This decorative cloth would have been used to cover the bargehouse or cabin and was to shelter the passengers before the custom of having a hard roof which, besides giving shelter, could accommodate additional passengers.

In 1681 Mr Fritton of Windsor supplied a barge and two wherries for £5 10s. This cost included the men's breakfast and dinner, fetching the Company banner and streamers and taking them back to the Hall. The following year, Mr Peter Rich, Liveryman, was one of the Sheriffs and no doubt the Company would have been represented in the procession on the Thames. In 1736 wooden pegs are mentioned to hang the barge cloth at the upper end of the Hall. New silk banners bearing the City Arms, the Royal Standard, Union flag, the Company Arms and those of Frederick Prince of Wales were bought in 1832, when Sir Peter Laurie, Saddler, was Lord Mayor. He embarked at the Tower of London in the State barge with twenty-four oarsmen for Westminster, returning to Blackfriars to complete his procession on land. In 1845 the Company had another Sheriff – John Laurie, MP for Newport and a Common Councilman. This would have been an occasion when the Company may have hired a barge.

Although many of the Company's treasures were lost in a fire caused by enemy action in 1940, the funeral pall of 1508, the silver plate and quarterage purse were in a place of safety and survived. There is also a banner with the Company arms painted on silk, approximately 4ft by 6ft, with a fringe of the Company colours, blue and gold. This was made by Tutill of City Road in 1911 to hang in the Guildhall. It would be similar in design to the type of flag or banner flown at the stern of the Company barge on ceremonial occasions.

The quarterage purse of the Saddlers' Company

The Saddlers' flag made in 1911 to hang in the Guildhall

Part of the Saddlers' Company funeral pall, dated 1508

THE CARPENTERS' COMPANY (26)

THE EARLIEST REFERENCE to the Carpenters occurs in the City records of 1271, and the Book of Ordinances drawn up in 1333 which indicates the principal objects of the Brotherhood. A copy of the Book, made in 1388, is held in the Public Record Office. A grant of Arms was made in 1466. Their first Charter was granted by Edward IV in 1477. The Arms depict a chevron between three pairs of dividers representing instruments of the carpenter's craft. The motto is 'Honour God'. The patron saint of the Company appears to be the Virgin Mary and is believed to have been chosen because she was the Mother of Him who was known on earth as The Carpenter's Son.

There is no record of the Carpenters owning a barge but there are references to a barge being hired for State occasions. The first of these was in 1455 for a procession to Westminster to accompany the Mayor. Again in 1460 and 1470 barges were hired but there are no details. In 1487 two barges were hired to meet King Henry VII (Henry Tudor, about two years after the Battle of Bosworth). The next occasion was to accompany Henry VII and Elizabeth of York, for her coronation as Queen, from Greenwich to Whitehall in 1486. In 1490 a barge was hired to attend Arthur, Prince of Wales, and in 1610 to attend another prince, Henry, Prince of Wales, from Richmond to Whitehall.

In 1547 there is an account of Moule the Shipwright being paid 14s for a barge to Westminster, when Sir John Gresham, Mercer, founder of a Grammar School at Holt, Norfolk, was Lord Mayor. In 1662 the Carpenters attended the procession and pageant to celebrate the marriage of Charles II and Catherine of Braganza. The barge and music together cost £18 11s 6d.

During the period in which ceremonial barges were in use the Carpenters had a Lord Mayor, Sir William Staines, in 1800. This was a momentous year in which Nelson arrived back in London after the Battle of the Nile and he took part in the Lord Mayor's Day celebrations by having lunch with Sir William. The Carpenters were elected as Sheriffs in 1711 (Sir John Cass), 1726 (Sir William Ogborne), 1798 (Sir William Champion), 1846 (Robert Kennard) and 1849 (William Lawrence MP). The Company would almost certainly have taken part in processions on the Thames to Westminster in these years.

The Hall was completely destroyed by enemy action in 1940 and no artefacts have survived from a barge. However, there is a painting by Sir Frank Brangwyn of the Court embarking in a barge, commissioned in 1912 by William Cobay the then Master. The Carpenters have a banner of the Company Arms painted on silk. This is approximately 4ft by 6ft and was commissioned to hang in the Guildhall in 1911.

*The Carpenters' Arms on a silk flag commissioned to
hang in the Guildhall in 1911*

The Cordwainers' Company (27)

The Cordwainers are first mentioned as a trade guild in 1087. They embraced several branches of the leather industry including the girdlers, tanners, curriers and leathersellers. In the reign of Edward III the Cordwainers were of sufficient wealth and influence to rank fifteenth in the list of thirty-two Companies, which gave gifts to the King to support the war in France. Ordinances for their better government were drawn up and approved by the Lord Mayor in 1271. An ordinance was passed by Henry IV in 1409 to settle the differences between 'cobblers' (workers in old leather) and 'cordwainers' (workers in new leather). Henry VI granted the Company its first Charter in 1439 which gave the Cordwainers complete control over the tanning of leather and making of shoes in the City and for two miles around. The Cordwainers received a grant of Arms in June 1579, which depicts a gold chevron between three goats' heads horned and bearded. The goat's head also forms the crest referring to the source of the original skins which the Cordwainers worked. The motto is 'Corio et arte' (With leather and skill).

There is no history of the Company owning a barge but they may well have hired or shared one when one of their Liverymen was a Sheriff. In 1272, Richard de Paris, Cordwainer, was one of the Sheriffs. Although this was before the processions commenced it demonstrates that the Company was of some importance at the time. There is no record of another Sheriff until John Wheelton in 1839, when he and his companion Sheriff were committed to custody by the House of Commons for an alleged breach of privileges. Thomas Cotterell became a Sheriff in 1851.

There is a badge now worn by the Beadle which is believed to be the Bargemaster's badge and is referred to as such in the company's history. It is smaller than the average badge but of a similar design. It was purchased at auction in 1956 and appears to date from about 1580. A banner 4ft by 6ft which is in store at the Museum of London, is complete with flag pole and bears the Company Arms painted on silk. This is one of the banners commissioned to hang in the Guildhall in 1911. A similar flag could have been flown on a hired barge.

The Cordwainers' Arms on a silk flag with flag pole for the Guildhall in 1911

The Cordwainers' Bargemaster's badge c.1580, now worn by the Beadle

THE PAINTER STAINERS' COMPANY (28)

THE EARLIEST extant Ordinances of the Painters date from 1283. The originals are in Norman-French and were to be observed by all good men of the Craft. Four men were appointed in 1328 to govern the craft. The fraternity was of a religious nature and was dedicated to St Luke. Services were held at the Church of St Giles, Cripplegate, for all members of the craft. The Painters and the Stainers joined to form one company in 1502. The Company received a Grant of Arms in 1486 and its first Charter from Elizabeth I in 1581. The Arms depict a chevron between three phoenix heads with the phoenix as a crest. The spotted panthers as supporters were added at a later date. The motto is 'Amor et obedientia' (Love and obedience), originally 'Amor queat obedientam'. The supporters and motto were recognised at the visitation of 1530. A full Charter and licence in mortmain was granted by Queen Elizabeth in 1581. The new Grant of Arms for the joined Companies (Painters and Stainers) was confirmed by Rouge Dragon in 1588, showing each Arms quartered. The Company reverted to its original Arms in 1972.

John Dessent, Sergeant Painter to Charles I, sometime between 1625 and 1649 was concerned with 'painting and gilding the Pryvie [Royal] Barge'. This included the figures of Justice and Fortitude. The barge had thirty-six oars and must have been one of the largest of all the Royal barges. The Painters appear to have owned their own barge in 1671, when there is a reference in the Company archives, held at the Guildhall, to Mr Saunders being asked 'to make two scutcheons for the barge in the room of those that are wanting'. There are also references to hiring a barge but no details. In 1673 there was no 'going by water on Lord Mayor's Day' but instead a dinner was provided at the Hall for members of the Company and their wives, the charge being 2s 5d per head. In 1681 the Company proceeded by water to Westminster on Lord Mayor's day. The Dyers' barge was hired for £6 10s with all necessaries and four watermen to carry the banners from landing to the Hall. The Company's 'wast' cloths were to be hung round the barge and their banner hung upon it, and no watermen were to dine at the Hall except the four that carried the banners. In 1806 when Jonathan Miles became a Sheriff the Company hired a barge with the Dyers' Company, the other Sheriff, James Branscombe, being a Dyer. On Lord Mayor's Day the two Companies met at the London Tavern and marched to the Guildhall, where the Lord Mayor joined the procession. The party drove to Blackfriars Bridge where they took to the water and proceeded to Palace Yard, Westminster to take their oaths. In September 1830 another member of the Painters, Sir William Henry Poland, who was also Master of the Company was elected Sheriff. The other Sheriff was Chapman Marshall, an Innholder, who became Lord Mayor in 1839. The two Companies shared a barge for the procession by water to Westminster.

The Company had banners for use on a hired barge which were preserved and said to be hanging in their Hall when their history was compiled in 1923. Unfortunately these banners have not survived, but a banner commissioned to hang in the Guildhall in 1911 which has the full Arms of the Company painted on silk has been restored and is exhibited in the Museum of London. Also, as the Scriveners' Company do not have a Hall of their own, the Painters display two flags for them. These are mounted on a stand covered by glass. One is the full Arms and the other the Crest of the Scriveners' Company. The flags are 4ft by 6ft painted on silk in very good colours.

*The Painter Stainers' flag with the combined Company arms
commissioned in 1911 to hang in the Guildhall*

The Fraternity of Innholders existed in the City in 1473 and Ordinances were approved in 1483. The Company was incorporated in 1514 by Charter. A Charter was granted by Charles II in 1663; the Company at this time was titled The Fraternity of Innholders of St Julian le Herberger, St Julian being their patron saint. The Charter applied to all persons who held, kept, or occupied an inn, 'hostry', 'petty ostry', or livery stable, in the City of London or within three miles of the same. The Company prospered and was able to contribute £500 towards the Dutch Wars of Charles II, without having to sell any of their silver, as did some of the other Companies. The Company was granted Arms in 1634 which depict a chevron between three oatsheaves and a St Julian cross, supported by a horse on either side. The oatsheaves represent the staple sustenance provided by the innholder for the traveller's horse. The crest is a gold star appearing out of a cloud; the motto is 'Hinc spes affulget' (Hope shines from here).

The Innholders took part in the procession and pageant to escort Queen Catherine from Hampton Court to Whitehall in August 1662. A barge was hired and dressed with a cloth and ribbons. The cost included £3 10s for the bargemen and £3 1s 6d for the musicians. Expenses for food were: six stones of beef to boil and three stones to roast 18s 6d, lamb 6s 6d, eighteen chickens 18s, two dozen bottles of sack, one dozen bottles of claret £2 16s 4d, and beer 19s 4d. It is not clear if this refreshment was all consumed on the barge or at the Hall before departure. In 1664 there is an instance of hiring a barge, when the cost was £4 15s. The occasion is not specified but may have been for a procession to Westminster. The Company took part in a number of processions in their own barge. However, in 1667 they sent their regrets to join the Lord Mayor's procession, the reason being the heavy cost of rebuilding their Hall after the Great Fire of 1666.

Sir Chapman Marshall, Liveryman, was elected Sheriff in 1830 and Lord Mayor in 1839. David William Wire, Liveryman, was elected Sheriff in 1853 and Lord Mayor in 1858. Two other Liverymen were also elected Sheriffs – Richard Peck in 1832 and Henry Muggeredge in 1854. It is very probable that the Innholders would have hired a barge to escort these gentlemen to Westminster for their oath takings.

This Company has a flag 4ft by 6ft with their Arms painted on silk. It is one of those commissioned to hang in the Guildhall in 1911. It has been in store with others at the Museum of London and is now waiting to be restored and hung in the Innholders' Hall.

*The Innholders' flag with the Company Arms
made to hang in the Guildhall*

*The Innholders' Arms of 1670, without the cross of St Julian,
from the ceiling of the Court Room*

THE FOUNDERS' COMPANY (33)

THE FIRST MENTION of the Fraternity of Founders, or Coppersmiths, is a grant of Ordinances for the management of the craft in the reign of Edward III in 1365. The goods made of brass and brass alloys were mostly candlesticks, buckles, spurs, stirrups, pots, ewers and basins. In 1376 the guild had the right to send two representatives to the Common Council. The Founders also had the right of assizing all small brass weights in the City and within three miles. These powers were confirmed by a corporation Order in 1587. The Company received a Grant of Arms in 1590 which depicts a laverpot between two taper candlesticks, examples of the founder's art. The Crest is a fiery furnace from which a melting-pot is being lifted by a pair of tongs held by two arms emerging from the clouds. The motto is 'God the only Founder'. A Royal Charter was granted by James I in 1614.

There are several references in the Company archives, held at the Guildhall, to the hiring of a barge, mostly for escorting the Lord Mayor and Sheriffs to Westminster but without many details. In 1498, 32s 4d was paid for making banners. In 1540 a barge was hired for a pageant which was probably to celebrate the marriage of Anne of Cleves to Henry VIII. Another barge was hired in 1559 to escort Queen Elizabeth from Westminster to the Tower. In 1677 new banners were purchased for £30 which was said to be twice the cost in 1626. At one time the Company had the rights to Swan Upping, but these were sold in 1590 (probably to the Dyers' Company).

A carving of the Arms of the Founders' Company

THE POULTERERS' COMPANY (34)

THE POULTERERS existed as a guild in the fourteenth century. Ordinances were granted in 1368, 1440, 1530, 1543 and 1550. The Company received a Charter in 1504 though the first recorded Charter of Incorporation is dated 1665. The Company was granted Arms in 1634 which depict a blue chevron with three swans, between three cranes. A stork with expanded wings forms the crest, and pelicans wounding their own breasts stand as supporters. The swans, cranes and storks represent the merchandise of the poulterer; the pelican is an emblem of the Eucharist and symbolises charity. Their motto is 'Remember your oath'. The Poulterers exercised a very strict control over their members' code of conduct and price control. Short weight meant being put in the stocks or dragged on a hurdle through the streets with the offending goods round your neck; the most severe punishment was being deprived of your living in the City. The nearest city which would accept you then was Coventry, hence the phrase 'sent to Coventry'.

The Company hired a barge to take part in escorting Queen Catherine from Hampton Court to Whitehall in August 1662. It was decorated with a cloth and forty-three yards of ribbon which would have been of the Company colours – white and blue. Members were entertained by musicians and enjoyed refreshments. The Company also attended the Lord Mayor to Westminster by barge in October 1649, the year Charles I was executed. (On most other occasions the Company remained on land to help line the Lord Mayor's route.) The Lord Mayor who took office, Thomas Foot, Grocer, was knighted by Cromwell. He was displaced as an Alderman on the restoration of Charles II. In 1854 Charles Decimus Crosley, Liveryman, was elected Sheriff and the Company may well have hired a barge to accompany him to Whitehall.

The Company has a banner, recently restored at the Textile Conservation Centre at Hampton Court. It bears the full Company Arms painted on silk and is approximately 4ft by 6ft. It is exhibited at Livery Dinners.

The Poulterers' Arms on a silk flag before restoration

THE FIRST MENTION of the Cook's Company in the City was in 1379 when they were forbidden to sell victuals before 10 o'clock in the morning. The Cooks obtained incorporation from Edward IV with their first charter in July 1482. Arms were granted in October 1467 which depict a chevron between three blue columbine flowers. The crest, a cock pheasant, and supporters, a buck and doe, were granted in 1614. The motto is 'Vulnerati non victi' (Wounded but not conquered). The columbine probably represents a form of ginger which was once used for culinary purposes, partly for flavour and partly for preserving.

Two Liverymen were elected Sheriff, Samuel Russel in 1731, and Samuel Birch in 1811, who became Lord Mayor in 1814. When Birch processed to Westminster the Company hired a barge for forty persons with banners, one of which bore his Arms. During his term of office he welcomed the Duke of Wellington after the victory at Waterloo in 1815. The Company has a reproduction of an old banner bearing the Company arms.

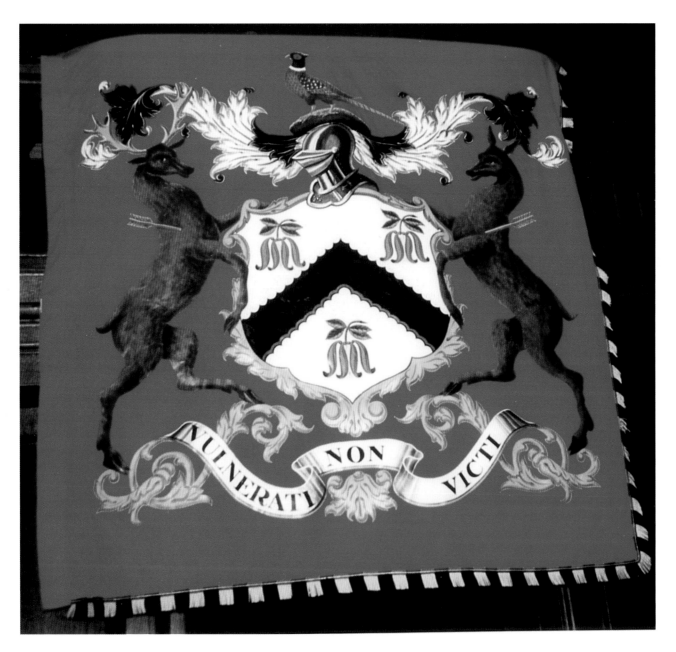

The Cooks' Arms on a modern banner

THE COOPERS' COMPANY (36)

THE COOPERS were granted ordinances by the Court of Aldermen in 1396. These were renewed in 1409 and again in 1420 when they were required to mark all barrels with their own sign which had to be recorded at the Guildhall. Their first Charter was granted in 1501. Eight years later they received a Grant of Arms, of which there was a re-exemplification in 1909. The arms depict three annulets and a royne between two broad axes, and three lilies slipped, stalked and leaved. The crest is a demi-heathcock with a blue body decorated with gold annulets holding in its beak a lily. The supporters are on either side a camel, decorated with annulets and bridled. The motto is 'Love as Brethren'. The royne and broad axe were two of the cooper's tools; the annulets were symbols of the hoops of a cask.

In 1509 the Coopers took part in the funeral procession of Henry VII on the River Thames. In 1533 the Company attended Anne Boleyn from Greenwich to the Tower by water, following her marriage to Henry VIII and as part of the ceremonies of her recognition as Queen. (Only three years later she made another journey to the Tower to be imprisoned and later executed.) In 1540 the Company attended Anne of Cleves when a barge was 'decorated with a blue cloth and hung with 14 emblazoned shields.' A musician was hired for 3s 4d and 8s 7d was spent on refreshments. Most of the early barges that were available for hiring were quite small. In 1584 a vessel with only six oarsmen was hired by the Company on Lord Mayor's day for 26s 8d. In 1609 the Company hired a barge to accompany Prince Henry from Whitehall to Chelsea for his installation as Prince of Wales. In 1662 a barge was purchased for £178 10s; it required a mate and fourteen oarsmen when it was in use. At the same time a Bargemaster was appointed. In 1683 the Company exchanged a barge-house with the Vintners. Three years later a second barge was built.

In 1688 John Fleet, Liveryman, was elected Sheriff. He became Lord Mayor in 1692, having translated to the Grocers' Company. A third barge was built in 1718 costing £382. In 1740 Sir Daniel Lambert was Lord Mayor, having

A quarter badge from the Coopers' Company barge

been Sheriff in 1733. In order to take this office he had to translate to the Vintners' Company. The Coopers had another Lord Mayor, Sir Robert Willimot in 1742, who made history by being the first Sheriff to refuse to translate to one of the Great Twelve Companies in order to become Lord Mayor. The Company barge would have been put to good use in transporting Liverymen to Westminster on these occasions. By 1774 the barge was out of repair and no longer fit for use. The Company decided against building a new one and from then on shared or hired a barge.

In 1777 the Company had another Lord Mayor, Sir James Esdaile, a banker, who had been a Sheriff in 1766. On this occasion a barge was hired from the Tallow Chandlers' Company. The same barge was hired for two other Mayors – Thomas Johnson in 1840 and for David Salomons in 1855. For the procession flags and banners were carried on the barge, including a French Tricolour with the Union Jack in the centre, emblematic of the alliance with France in the Crimean War (1853–6.)

Two ornaments from the barge are preserved in the Court Room. They are both shields, probably quarter badges to be fixed on either side of the stern, and both have the Arms of the Company in the centre. One shield has more elaborate carving round the Arms than the other and has the crest at the top and the carving of a face at the base. It is possible that this one was carried on the bow of a hired barge. Larger Arms with supporters would normally decorate the stern.

A carving of the Coopers' Arms with the crest,
possibly from the bow of a barge

THE FOUNDATION of the Fraternity of Tylers and Bricklayers may be as early as the middle of the thirteenth century. Until then all the houses in London were thatched. Tiles were introduced to limit the risk of fire. To encourage the change, fines were often imposed in the form of tiles instead of cash. In 1245 an order was published by the Mayor that all houses in the main thoroughfares should be covered with tiles or slates. In spite of the importance of their craft there is no reference to the Tylers and Bricklayers before the fourteenth century and they did not obtain a charter until 1568. This specifies a common seal, a licence in mortmain, the levy of fines and correction of bad workmanship over a radius of fifteen miles. A Grant of Arms was made in 1569. The original patent has not survived but the Arms were recorded at a visitation in 1634. These depict a fleur-de-lis, a symbol of the Blessed Virgin Mary, between two brick-axes, symbolising the craft, and a brush – a heraldic device representing roof tiling laths. The motto is 'In God is all our trust, let us never be confounded'.

In 1774, Sir William Plomer, Liveryman, was elected Sheriff; he became Lord Mayor in 1781. The Company probably hired or shared a barge on both these occasions. The Company shared a barge with the Goldsmiths' Company in 1793 for the procession to Westminster – the Lord Mayor and one Sheriff were Goldsmiths, the other Sheriff was C. Hamerton, a Tyler and Bricklayer.

No artefacts have survived, which is not unusual for Companies which used only hired barges. Flags and banners seem to have survived more often than anything else.

The Arms of the Tylers' and Bricklayers' Company

THE BLACKSMITHS' COMPANY (40)

EDWARD II incorporated the Blacksmiths by ancient prescription in 1325. Their first Articles were approved by the Mayor and Aldermen in 1372. Although blacksmith-spurriers (makers of spurs) were virtually a separate guild, their work was closely supervised by the blacksmiths and the two were combined into one guild by the Charter of Queen Elizabeth I in 1571 under the name of Blacksmiths. Other specialist blacksmiths such as locksmiths and clocksmiths were never separate bodies. However there was considerable conflict between the clockmakers and the rest of the Blacksmiths which lasted until the Clockmakers were granted their own Charter in 1631; they are now the best of friends.

The Blacksmiths' first Grant of Arms was made in 1490. In 1610 a new Grant was made, which depicts a chevron or between three crowned hammers on a field of sable, the crest with a phoenix standing upon a hill firing herself with the sun's beams. The motto is 'By hammer and hand all arts do stand'. In 1990 there was a further Grant of Arms to include the supporters. There is no history of the Company owning or hiring a barge. However, in 1789 Thomas Baker, Liveryman, was elected Sheriff and this would have been an occasion when the Company might have hired a barge. The Company does have a long banner or pennant dating from the mid 19th century, the end of which has been damaged by water. It is said that due to their great length, such banners may have trailed in the water on the occasion of a procession on the Thames. The Company has two other flags consisting of the Royal Arms and the Company Arms; and another banner, which has not been clearly identified, that includes a Union Jack, a Regimental banner depicting a sword, a pike, two cannons, drums and a shield with a helm. This could be a banner belonging to Thomas Baker as it also has swans' heads and necks and wheat ears; the latter are not often met with but they do occur in the arms of Baker. The Blacksmiths did raise and arm a band of Yeomen so it may be the Blacksmiths' Yeomanry banner.

The Blacksmiths' 19th-century long banner or pennant

*One of the Blacksmiths' flags, in need of restoration
showing St George and the dragon*

THE JOINERS' AND CEILERS' COMPANY (41)

THE JOINERS are known to have existed as a fraternity associated with the Church of St James Garlickhythe in 1375. In 1400 a petition was submitted by the Joiners and Carvers to the civic authority to appoint Wardens to control the craft and maintain standards of work and conduct. By-laws were formally ratified in 1575. Arms were granted in August 1571 which depict a chevron between two dividers extended points downwards, and a globe, with an escallop between two red roses. The original motto was 'God grant us to use justice with mercy' but was changed in 1769 to 'Join loyalty and liberty'.

The first Joiner to become Mayor of London was William de Joynier in 1239, having been Sheriff in 1222. He assisted in building Grey Friars' Church. This would have been long before the Mayor's processions on the Thames commenced and before the Fraternity of Joiners or Fusteers, as they were sometimes called, was recognised. Other Sheriffs followed – Charles Hopton in 1708, John Wilkes in 1771 (Lord Mayor in 1774), Watkin Lewes in 1772 (Lord Mayor in 1780 as Sir Watkin), and Richard Clark in 1777 (Lord Mayor in 1784). When Sir Watkin was a Sheriff in 1772, the Company hired the Drapers' barge. In 1780 and 1784 there was no barge large enough to contain the Livery and the Company walked on Lord Mayor's Day.

The Company has a banner dated by the Textile Conservation Centre at Hampton Court to about 1840, showing the Company Arms granted in 1571. This is probably a copy of an earlier flag.

The Joiners' Company banner during restoration at Hampton Court

THE WEAVERS' COMPANY (42)

THE WEAVERS are one of the oldest guilds, their date of incorporation being 1184. The Company still possess a Charter dated *c.*1155 of Henry II, confirming one granted by Henry I which would be dated 1135 at the latest. The 1155 charter is the earliest surviving charter for a guild. The guild was quite powerful and came into conflict with King John. Edward III gave a considerable boost to foreign trade by inviting foreign weavers to settle in England. The guild eventually combined with the Flemish and Brabant weavers in 1498. The Company has a number of Charters and is unique in being governed by a Charter of Queen Anne. The reason for its position of forty-second in order of precedence seems to be its lack of wealth when the order was finally decided in 1516.

The first mention of a barge appears to be when John Johnson was appointed Bargemaster to the Company in 1611 to replace John Spricklett 'lately deceased' – 'He

[Johnson] was to provide a hired barge for Lord Mayor's Day at a cost of 40*s*, whereof he hath received 10*s* in part and the Court have given him 12*d* in earnist.' In addition four whifflers were chosen and two men to serve as drum and fife at 5*s* each for the day. In October 1618 two watermen were engaged to serve the Company for 50*s* with a convenient barge for the Livery. The next year Richard Jones, a freeman of the Company, apparently working as waterman, was to provide a convenient barge for Lord Mayor's Day. The custom is described as processing to the stairs at the river side, with the Bailiffs, Officers and Livery of the Company wearing their gowns. The pensioners, drums, fifes and trumpeters and men carrying the banners processed wearing scarves of the Company colours of blue and yellow. The Company then took to their barge, the stern of which carried the Company Arms carved, painted and gilded, with the Company banner flying above. It was

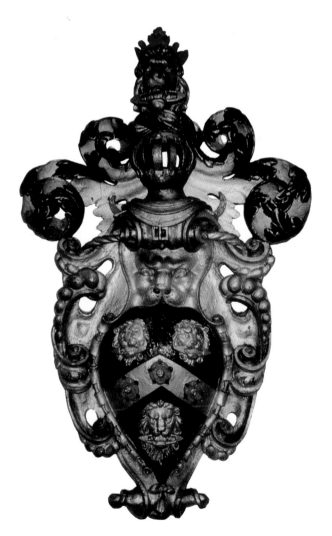

The Arms of the Weavers' Company, which may have formed the bow badge of a barge

customary to have a mythical figure at the prow; the Weavers may have had a leopard with a shuttle in his mouth. The rudder may have been decorated with the painting of a dolphin. The barge would have proceeded upstream to Westminster, accompanied by music and saluted on the way by several peals of ordnance. At the landing stage a guard normally formed a lane to Westminster Hall.

On the return voyage the Lord Mayor's party would make for Baynard's Castle, and the Companies' barges to St Paul's Steps and other landing places, to process to St Paul's and finally to the Guildhall. Feasting would have taken place on the barges. For instance, the Weavers are known to have had ten gallons of Canary wine and twenty dozen cakes available on their barge. Afterwards the Lord Mayor would dine at Guildhall and the various Companies would retire to their own halls for a feast. The expenses for the day were quite considerable. In 1687 they amounted to £79 11s 8d for the Weavers' Company. In 1671 and 1672 the Company hired two barges, one for the Livery and one for the musicians.

In 1673 the Weavers had a barge built by John Graves for £115, including eighteen oars. The barge was 72ft long with a beam of 11ft. Banners painted on silk by Edmond Pickering were supplied at a cost of £75; painting and gilding cost a further £55, making a total of £250. Two long coats in blue satin were supplied for the Bargemaster and steersman together with twenty caps and eighteen white linen waistcoats, with the Weavers' arms on tin badges for the crew at a cost of £11. The Weavers rented a bargehouse at Chelsea. This was built by the Tallow Chandlers on land rented from the Apothecaries and sublet to the Weavers, who paid them £9 towards the building of the bargehouse and a rent of £1 10s a year. The Bargemaster received £2 a year and eighteen watermen shared £5.

The barge was occasionally used for purposes other than the processions on Lord Mayor's day. In October 1710, the barge was allowed to go to Brentford to carry friends to vote for Esquire Barker and Mr Austin, both Parliamentary candidates. The cost of running their own barge eventually became too great, and in 1737 the Weavers gave up their lease of the bargehouse at Chelsea and sold the barge to be broken up. The barge cloth, banners and streamers were put into store. In 1770 William Baker, a member of the Company, was elected Sheriff but there is no record of a barge being hired or shared. In 1833, when Samuel Wilson was a Sheriff, the Company hired a barge which they shared with the Spectacle Makers who provided the other Sheriff. When Samuel Wilson became Lord Mayor in 1838, he travelled to Westminster in the City barge, but the Weavers' procession went by land to save the expense of hiring a barge.

The Company still has six banners which have been deposited on permanent loan with the Museum of London. They consist of a pennant or streamer, which is 24ft long by 4ft 6in. at the hoist. This depicts the Company Arms granted in 1490: three red roses on a chevron between three leopards' heads each holding a shuttle in its mouth, with dragons as supporters and a crowned leopard with a shuttle in its mouth as the crest. The motto is 'Weave truth with trust'. The other flags are the Royal Arms, the City Arms, a full Coat of Arms of the Company, the Arms of Alderman Wilson and one with Arms not identified. These flags are all approximately 4ft by 6ft and are believed to date from 1838 when Samuel Wilson was Lord Mayor. The long streamer may be older and could date from c.1750. The Company has a Bargemaster's badge and a bow badge showing the Weavers' Arms and crest. They also still have two coats believed to have belonged to the crew.

The Weavers' long banner or pennant,
believed to date from 1750

The Weavers' Bargemaster's badge

A jacket belonging to a member of the barge's crew

THE SCRIVENERS' COMPANY (44)

THE ORIGINAL SCRIVENERS were confidential writers of legal documents such as wills and deeds, and from 1392 were Notaries granted Faculties by the Archbishop of Canterbury – as is still the case today. The Scriveners' Company was formally established as a Livery Company of the City of London by Ordinances granted by the Mayor and Aldermen on 26 September 1373. It was granted a Royal Charter of Incorporation by James I on 28 January 1617. The Company was granted Arms on 11 November 1634. Its Arms are a blue field on which is a gold spread eagle, holding in its beak a penner (pen case) and ink-bottle, standing upon a red book with gold clasps. The supporters on each side of the shield are Counsellors (Barristers)-at-Law in early seventeenth century dress. The crest is a hand holding a quill pen, issuing from a cloud, over which is a scroll bearing the motto 'Scribite Scientes' (Write, ye Learned Ones). This, most unusually, is repeated below the shield and supporters.

In 1671, Sir Robert Clayton, Alderman and Sheriff, became Master of the Scriveners Company. He was Lord Mayor in 1679–80, after translating to the Drapers' Company.

The Company had another Sheriff in 1803, Sir James Shaw, who became Lord Mayor in 1805. By this time it was no longer necessary to be a member of the Great Twelve Companies to hold the high office of Lord Mayor. It is most likely that on each of these occasions the Company would have shared or hired a barge for a procession on the Thames to Whitehall.

The Company still has a long pennant or streamer (20ft 10ins long) which, as the Scriveners have had no Hall of their own since the Great Fire of 1666, is exhibited at the Stationers' Hall. The pennant shows the Union Jack, the City Arms, the City crest with sword and mace and the Scriveners' crest. The Union Jack is folded to reduce the length of the banner for display. There are also two flags belonging to the Scriveners exhibited at the Hall of the Painters' Company. These are of the Company Arms and of the Company crest. Three other flags – a pre-1801 Royal Standard, the City Arms, and the Union Flag – are in store. A full description of these flags, made by the Victoria and Albert Museum in 1983, is held by the Company. It is probable that a few, if not all, of these flags were used on a hired barge at some time.

The Scriveners' long banner exhibited at the Stationers' Hall

*The Arms of the Scriveners' Company on a silk flag
exhibited at the Painter Stainers' Hall*

The Stationers' Company (47)

THE STATIONERS existed as a Fraternity or Guild of text writers and limners (or decorators of manuscripts) for some time before they obtained the authority of the Court of Aldermen to elect Wardens and to make rules for the government of their Brotherhood in 1403. They were incorporated by Queen Mary and obtained their first Charter in 1556. The Company was granted Arms in September 1557 which depict an eagle between two roses on a chevron between three books, with wings issuing out of a cloud radiated; an eagle with wings expanded with a diadem above its head perched on a book is the crest. The motto is 'Verbum Domini manet in aeternum' (The word of God endureth for ever).

The word 'stationer' originated in the universities and was attached to those who made and sold books and writing materials from fixed ('stationery') stalls in contrast to pedlars and itinerant salesmen. After the Company's incorporation in 1557, it was given powers to search for, seize and destroy heretical and seditious works, and to license, together with a government licenser, those that were harmless.

Sir Thomas Davies became the Company's first Sheriff in 1666 and Lord Mayor in 1676, after translating to the Drapers' Company. Sir Thomas was described by Pepys as 'the little fellow, the bookseller, my school fellow, and now a Sheriff, which is a strange turn, methinks'. Although the Stationers were never a wealthy company they have produced eleven Lord Mayors to date, who have included Swift's friend and printer, John Barber, in 1732, and the paper merchant, Sir John Key, who was Lord Mayor two years running in 1831 and 1832. In addition they have produced six sheriffs who did not achieve the office of Lord Mayor.

The Company has a book, *The State Barges of The Stationers' Company 1680–1850*, which contains a great deal of information and a number of illustrations. The Stationers first hired a barge in 1662 to take part in the procession on the Thames in honour of Catherine of Braganza. The Company owned six barges, the first built in 1679 at a cost of £187. The fifth was built by Roberts in 1790 for £807 2s and the last by Searle in 1826 for £1,785. In 1680 the Bargemaster was paid a salary of £4 and the mate £2. The watermen were paid by the day, when required; in addition the Bargemaster was paid 12d and the mate 8d for their dinner, when the barge was in use. The Bargemaster also had a new coat every two years.

The Bargemaster's badge is on display at Stationers' Hall and is in perfect condition. There is also a splendid model of their last barge (see page 154). The Stationers have a small painting of a barge with six oars at Richmond and a print of eights at Oxford with Livery barges in the background. There is a coat of very light silk in blue and gold which may have belonged to a member of the barge crew or a musician. A rosette has also survived of the type which could have been worn by members of the Company who were not entitled to Livery or who did not possess a gown. Exhibited in the Hall is a very long banner or pennant belonging to the Scriveners' Company, who do not have a Hall of their own, and a fully-laden barge is depicted in one of the stained-glass windows.

A window in the Stationers' Hall showing the Company barge

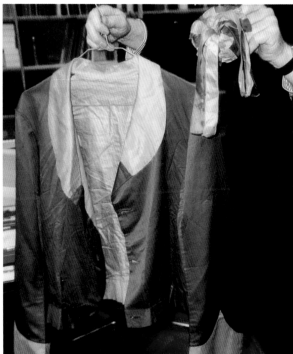

The Stationers' Bargemaster's badge

A coat belonging to an oarsman or musician, and a rosette

This Policy of Assurance Witnesseth, That

The Worshipful Company of Stationers,

ha ... paid the Sum of ... Shilling
to the PHŒNIX ASSURANCE-COMPANY of LONDON, and havi
be paid, to them at their Office in Lombard-Street, the Sum of Two Pou
on the 29 September 1796 and the like Sum ... Yearly, on
continuance of this Policy, FOR INSURANCE FROM LOSS OR DAMAGE BY F
the Sum or Sums hereinafter recited upon the Property herein defcribed, in
forth, and not elfewhere (unlefs allowed by Endorfement previoufly made
viz.—On

The Building of their two Barge Houses only adjoining with Loft over under one Roof situate near the Palace at Lambeth being Brick built Three Hundred Pounds.

And On their Barge in one of the above Barge Houses, or whilst on the River Thames Seven Hundred Pounds.

N.B. The former Policy of this Office N. 70,432 is agreed to be Cancelled, and made Void from and after the Commencement of this Policy.

An insurance policy with the Phoenix Assurance Company
for the Stationers' barge and bargehouse 1796

LITTLE IS KNOWN of the early history of the guild and its role in the development of English embroidery in the Middle Ages. In 1469 the Company is known to have equipped twelve men-at-arms to watch the City Gates and by this time must have been well-established. Their craft would have included making splendid vestments and altar-cloths, tapestry for kings and nobles, dresses for ladies, doublets for knights and adornments for swords. Some magnificent funeral palls are still preserved by a number of the Livery Companies. The Company was granted its first Charter by Elizabeth I in October 1561 and Arms were granted in August 1558. The Arms depict three lions of England passant gardant, two broches (a combined bodkin and spindle) and two quills of gold thread, supported by two lions. The crest is the Holy Dove upon a roundel radiated; the motto is 'Omnia desuper' (All things come from above). The Company eventually lost control over its craft and trade in 1710, but by no means lost interest in the art of embroidery.

The Broderers had one Sheriff in 1768, John Shakespear, when the Company may have processed to Westminster aboard a hired barge. The Broderers still have a banner or pennant 16ft long which escaped damage by enemy action in 1941. It is believed to date from early eighteenth century and is beautifully embroidered on blue silk. They also have a banner of the full Company arms approximately 4ft by 6ft from the late sixteenth century, which was damaged by enemy action in 1941. There are three other banners each bearing the Company arms with slight variations, all embroidered on blue silk. These may well have been used on a hired barge.

Two of three surviving banners, embroidered on blue silk with the Company Arms.
Both have two trundles in the lower corners. One is dated 1864

The Broderers' long banner or pennant

A flag with the Broderers' Arms, badly damaged

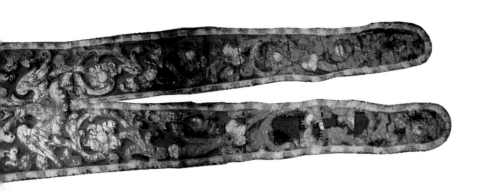

THE MUSICIANS' COMPANY (50)

THE MUSICIANS appear to have originated as a Society of Minstrels, known as the King's Minstrels, in April 1469 when they were granted a Royal Charter by Edward IV. Another Charter was granted by James I in 1604 which conveyed a common seal, a licence to mortmain and the privileges of making by-laws for the rule and government of the Mystery within three miles of London. Arms were granted in October 1604 which depict a swan with wings expanded within a double tressure flory counter-flory and a red rose between two lions passant gardant, with a lyre as the crest. The Royal emblems of the lion and the rose are explained by their origin as the King's Minstrals. As the Arms were granted in 1604, the feature of the tressure flory counter-flory of the Royal Arms of Scotland, marshalled with England by James VI of Scotland, indicate a compliment to the King.

The Fraternity took a prominent part in Tudor pageants and also taught singing and dancing. There is no doubt that they played an important part in entertainment on the City Livery barges, both during the processions to Westminster on Lord Mayor's Day and on many ceremonial and festive occasions. Nearly every Company employed three or four musicians (see Appendix II) who were quite well paid during voyages on the Thames. Their normal position on the barge was aft of the cabin, just in front of the helmsman. Occasionally a drummer is shown in paintings sitting on the end of the cabin top. On one occasion, in July 1717, a Company hired a whole barge for a complete band of fifty musicians. This would have been when Sir James Bateman, a Fishmonger, was Lord Mayor. The *Daily Courant* of 19 July 1717 reports that Handel's music was played. (Although Handel's Water Music was not published until 1740, it is believed that parts of the suite had already been composed.) It appears unusual to have a whole barge for musicians although the Weavers had a separate barge for musicians in 1671 and again in 1672. The Musicians had four Sheriffs – in 1764 Brass Crosby, in 1783 Sir Barnard Turner, in 1785 Sir Brook Watson (Lord Mayor in 1796), and in 1799 J. Blackhall.

The Company has one banner which replaces one destroyed in the Second World War.

The Musicians' Company Arms on a modern banner

The Turners' Company (51)

RINKING VESSELS of wood, turned on a lathe (the first machine tool), were the regular stock of early innholders, long before pewter and earthenware vessels were brought into regular use. One of the first references to Turners in the City is in a Pipe Roll of 1179. The Turners were in a position of some authority in 1310 when several Turners were sworn to make no other measures than gallons and quarts and no false measures, either for liquids or dry goods such as corn. In 1347 further restrictions were made in regard to the material of which they made their liquid measures. The wood was to be properly seasoned and they were to indicate regulation by marks on the bottom of each vessel. False vessels were to be burned in Cheapside. The Turners first and only known Charter was granted by James I in 1604. The licence in mortmain was conferred together with the right of search within five miles of London.

Arms were granted in December 1634 and depict a Catherine wheel between two columns with an imperial crown and a hatchet, with the figure of St Catherine crowned, wearing a mantle furred with ermine, holding a Catherine wheel and a sword, as the crest. The motto is 'By faith I obteigne'. The original guild was dedicated to St Catherine; the hatchet is an implement of the craft and the column a product.

The Turners has never been a wealthy company and none of its members seems to have been a Sheriff or Lord Mayor, though it appears that they must have taken part in at least one procession on the Thames as there is a reference in the Stationers' archives to a dispute with the Turners in 1678 regarding their place in the order of precedence with their barge. Perhaps Richard How, one of the Sheriffs and a Woodmonger, was also a member of their Company.

No artefacts relating to a barge have survived.

The Arms of the Turners' Company from a window in the Apothecaries' Hall

THE GLAZIERS' COMPANY (53)

THE GLAZIERS were not only craftsmen who set glass in windows but also glass painters. In early times the usual name for glaziers was 'verrers' and the first Ordinances were granted to the Verrers in February 1365. An early record of glass painting in this country is when St Benedict, Abbot of Wearmouth, sent for a French glass painter to fill the windows of his church, in AD 680. In the treaty of peace between Henry II and Philip of France at Tours in 1189, Philip was bound to allow one of his best glass painters to come to England. By 1328 a guild of Glass Painters was well established in London with a Master and one Warden. The Glaziers became in great demand and flourished. Edward III granted the Company livery. The Glaziers were incorporated in 1631 and were given control of their trade and the right to search by Act of Common Council in 1615. They received their first Charter from Charles I in 1638.

Their Arms were approved by Clarencieux, King of Arms, on a visitation in 1588. These Arms were certified in March 1926 and depict two grozing irons between four closing nails, and a demi-lion passant gardant supported on either side by a boy holding in the exterior hand a torch. The crest is a Lion's head, between two blue wings; the motto 'Lucem Da Nobis Deus' (Give us Thy Light O Lord). A grozing iron was used to shape glass by breaking off very small pieces with this special tool, before the use of a diamond. The closing nails held the glass in place until it fitted into the lead supporting the glass. The groove in the lead was then closed and the joins soldered. The Company has four identical banners or pennants, depicting the City Arms and the Company Arms. There is also a flag showing the Sovereign's Arms, which includes the White Horse of Hanover (c.1816–37) and another with the Company Arms. These are painted on silk and are approximately 4ft by 6ft. There is a reference to the purchase of new banners in 1753 in a Court book, held at the Guildhall. Although the Company did not have a Sheriff or Lord Mayor it appears that they did process on the Thames, in which case they would have had the banners to fly on a barge.

Three sections of one of four long banners, two of which are dated 1706 and two 1753

*One of the Glaziers' flags bears the Arms of George III,
the last King of England to use the fleur de lys*

THE APOTHECARIES had their origin in the Company of Pepperers who were well established in the City by 1180. The Pepperers dealt with spices and peppers and were in charge of the Great or King's Beam for weighing imported goods. Because they dealt 'en gros' they adopted the title of Grocer in 1373. There were already Apothecary Wardens in the Pepperers in 1328 and they eventually formed a separate section within the Grocers' Company. The Apothecaries were granted their own Charter by James I in 1617. The driving force in bringing this about was the Queen's Apothecary, Gideon de Laune. A Grant of Arms was made just six days after the Charter was received. These depict Apollo, the inventor of physic, with his head radiant, holding in his left hand a bow and in his right hand an arrow, supplanting a serpent, supported by two unicorns. The crest is a rhinoceros with its magical horn, which ground to a powder, was used as a medicine; the motto 'Opiferque per orbem dicor' (I am called throughout the world the bringer of aid) is from Ovid's *Metamorphoses*. The supporters, mythical unicorns (James I's 'special beasts'), may be a mark of Royal Favour. The serpent was originally drawn as a wyvern, a type of dragon emblematic of pestilence, which may have been to symbolise the struggle of medicine against disease. The helm is that of a peer which usually indicates a special honour, although it is not mentioned as such in the patent.

In 1631 the Apothecaries ordered their first barge to be hired from Athanasius Whyniard. It was to be 'a decent barge with watermen and a cloth to cover the barge, to carry at least fifty, to be provided with oars, a steersman, herbs and rushes and to fetch streamers and cushions, to find watermen their breakfast for £3 10s. By way of ernest he should receive 10s.' Additional expenses were – 'music £1 10s, ribbon for the members £2 6s, a barge cloth 5s, staves and boat hire for the young men 5s ["young men" being bachelors or yeomen]. Each Liveryman to pay 2s 6d to provide dinner on the day'. A Mr Taylor undertook to provide three banners, one with the King's Arms, another the City Arms and the third with the Company's Arms, also two long streamers with staves to bear them and rolling staves with paper to wrap them in, for which he was to receive £38. Hiring a barge continued for the next few years with very little variation in the expense.

In 1658 it was thought inconsistent with the dignity of the Society of Apothecaries to use a hired barge and the building of a Company barge was considered. Because of the expenses at the time of the Restoration of Charles II the scheme was not developed. In 1660 a barge was hired for £5 10s, which cost included 'light horsemen', small boats to help clear the way for the barge. A proposal for sharing a barge house with the Surgeons was discussed but came to nothing. Further expenses connected with the plague, the fire of London and rebuilding the Hall and chemical laboratory delayed the possibility of building a barge. In 1673, however, the Court decided to have a barge built and to purchase a bargehouse. An estimate was submitted by Nicholas Wheatley for £110, for a barge similar to that which he had supplied to the Mercers' Company in 1671, using the same carver, Richard Cleare. The contract is still in existence at the Guildhall in the Company archives. The Apothecaries were to have different carved work to include two unicorns on each side of the cabin door and a rhinoceros set over the same entrance. The Arms of the Company and the crest were to be set on the stern with screws so that these carvings could be removed and reset. A lease was arranged with Charles Chayne for land at Chelsea on which to build a bargehouse. Later this was to be developed into the famous Physic Garden where the Apothecaries grew herbs. They also instructed their apprentices in the garden, as well as taking them on herborising expeditions up river by barge. Some of the preparation of the herbs may have been carried out at their mill, which was said to be near to the garden, the final part of the preparation being at their factory at Black Friars. Drugs were sold from their warehouse on the premises. The Society had large contracts to supply drugs to the Army, the Navy and the East India Company.

In a description of the Company's second barge built in 1727, a great carved shield gilded and painted in the proper colours is mentioned. This could have been for the stern of the barge and would be very like the Arms of the Company over the entrance to the present Hall. Fluted pillasters with corinthian capitals are also mentioned, which would be similar to those shown in a photograph of the Merchant Taylors' barge, which was sold to one of the Oxford Colleges. The thwarts or seats and the oars were to be numbered, the oars being shorter towards the bow of the barge. (The oars of a Livery barge would appear rather clumsy today. In view of their length, the inboard end of each one was very thick and sometimes square in section to keep the oar in balance for the oarsmen.) In 1764 the barge was found to be past repair and a third barge was ordered from Charles Cowndell for £640. There is no doubt that all the barges were well used in frequent visits to Chelsea, as well as for ceremonial outings including Lord Mayor's Day, and also on social occasions. A few voyages were made to take troops down river to board troop ships. In 1790–1 when Sir Richard Carr Glyn was a Sheriff, the Salters' Company borrowed the Apothecaries' barge. Afterwards the Salters sent a letter of thanks enclosing ten guineas.

One of the important ceremonies in which the barge took part was for the funeral of Lord Nelson in 1806. This was an occasion when the Company flags (believed to have been purchased in 1797) were used; these are now exhibited in the Hall – two long streamers, or pennants, and two flags, one bearing the Company Arms and the other the figure of St Luke, the Patron Saint of Physicians. Two other flags of a similar size have not been restored. These represent the Royal Arms and the City Arms and are in store. The last procession to Westminster in which the barge took part was in 1816. By 1817 the barge was in a poor state and no longer safe to use. It was sold and the bargehouse let to Mr Lyall of the Swan Brewhouse. The two remaining bargehouses were let to the Goldsmiths' Company. The Apothecaries continued to use a hired barge for collecting herbs until c.1845. The Company Bargemaster had other duties besides those directly connected with the barge. On the Master's Day, in the morning, he took part in a procession to the Society's church, St Andrew by the Wardrobe, wearing his Bargemaster's coat and badge. He led the way with the Beadle who carried the Company mace or leading staff. After lunch the new Master would be installed after being crowned with a coronet. At a later date the Master and the Court would visit Chelsea by barge for a formal inspection of the Physic Garden.

The Company is fortunate in having a small carving of the Apothecaries Arms which was on their barge, probably on the barge house or cabin. There is also a plaque dated 1691, which was also on the barge. It has the initials of John Gover, the Master at that time, and the motto 'The Lord hath created medicine out of the earth' (Ecclesiasticus 28: 4). The Bargemaster's badge was lost soon after the last Bargemaster retired in 1817. Both the Arms and the plaque are displayed in the Court Room.

A plaque from the Apothecaries' barge with the initials
of John Gover, Master in 1691

*Sections of two long banners used on the Apothecaries' barge for
the funeral procession of Lord Nelson*

A flag with the Apothecaries' Arms

*A flag bearing the figure of St Luke,
the Patron Saint of Physicians*

*A large carving of the Apothecaries' Arms which could
have been on the stern of a barge*

To the Worsp.ll Company of Apothecaries

A Proposal for painting & gilding their barge by
Jn.º Goodyer.

The inside of the House being Wainscot to be Varnisht
The great carved shield gilded & painted in proper colours
The carved Trail boards gilded on each side
The waist board ornamented with the Kings, the City's
and Company's arms & crest with other embelishments.
a handsome Foliage fore & aft the sax boards.
The great Ogee of the Cornice round the house, the beads
round the sashes, & ornaments between ye pillasters gilt.
The Fluted Pillasters with Corinthian Chapiters and
bases, the beads round the pannels and fore bulk heads
and beads round ye doors all gilded.
Two large carved figures afore the house & two ditto
abaft gilded.
The four lower pannels of the fore bulk heads painted
with figures representing ye four seasons of the year.
The two upper pannells of the fore doors painted
with Apollo and Æsculapius.
The pannels of the two doors of the after bulk heads
painted with Hercules & Industry.
The great pannel of the after bulk head painted with
Neptune & Thetis in a chariot drawn by sea horses.
a Dolphin painted on the rudder
a mask head on the Transom

*Part of a proposal for painting the Apothecaries' barge
dated 1727*

The water gate at Chelsea Physic Garden

OPIFEROVE PER ORBEM DICOR

Arms from the cabin of the Apothecaries' barge

THE SHIPWRIGHTS were first mentioned in 1387 as a Fraternity in honour of St Simon and St Jude. Their Ordinances date from 1428 and their Charter from 1612 and 1784. There was another company called the Foreign Shipwrights but this was wiped out after a long struggle. Arms which had been granted to this company in 1605 were adopted by the Free Shipwrights in 1784. The Grant is in the possession of the Company with the Charter given by James I in April of 1605 and stored at the Guildhall. The Company did not have its own Charter until George V issued a Royal Warrant in 1920. The Arms depict the hull of a ship on the sea with a sword erect and a lion passant gardant lying on a red cross.

The crest is an ark resting upon a mount, upon which stands a dove bearing an olive branch, and with a sword in the prow of the ark. The motto is 'Within the ark safe for ever'.

The Shipwrights are not known to have owned or hired a barge themselves for processions on the Thames. However, they would have supplied barges to other Companies on festive and ceremonial occasions and would have been employed in building Company barges. In this way they would have been involved with all Livery Company occasions on the river. The Company owns an excellent model of a Livery barge, which may have been used as a 'traveller's sample'. This is now in the National Maritime Museum, Greenwich.

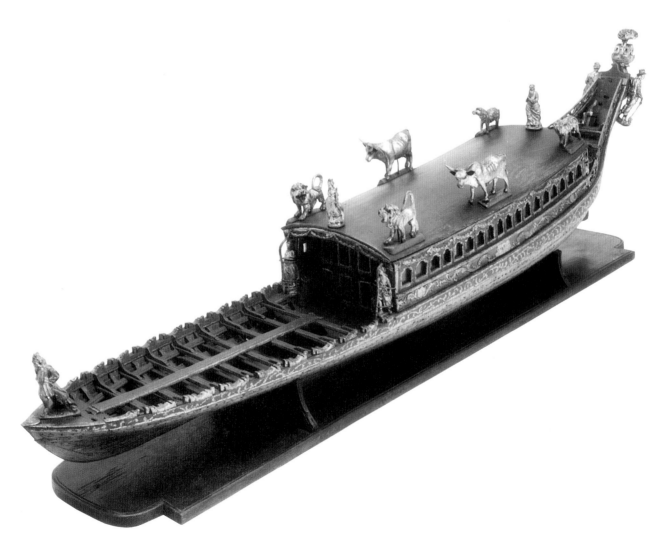

The Shipwrights' model barge

THE SPECTACLE MAKERS' COMPANY (60)

THE TRUE INVENTOR of spectacles does not appear to be known. They were sold by Haberdashers in the early fifteenth century in London, and when Caxton produced the first printed book in England *c.*1476, there was probably an increased demand for this aid. In a list of eighty-four trades in the City, from the early records of the Brewers' Company, spectacle-making is not included. The few craftsmen with this skill had not organised themselves into any sort of trade or guild. Robert Allt and fifteen London spectacle-makers, twelve of whom were members of the Brewers' Company, petitioned the King in Council for a Charter. This was granted by Charles I in 1629. The Grant of Livery was not obtained until 1809. Arms were granted in September 1950 and depict a chevron between three pairs of nose-spectacles with falcons charged with a sword erect as supporters. The crest depicts two arms holding a sun

in splendour within an annulet. The motto is 'A Blessing to the Aged'.

The Company had eighteen Sheriffs before 1856, of whom three became Lord Mayor. When James Harmer became a Sheriff in 1833 the Company shared a barge with the Weavers' Company; the other Sheriff, Samuel Wilson, being a member of the Weavers' Company. John Johnson was a Sheriff in 1836 and became Lord Mayor in 1845. Sir George Carroll, Sheriff in 1837, followed him as Lord Mayor in 1846. Sir James Duke was a Sheriff in 1836 and became Lord Mayor in 1848. A few years ago a chest was found in a cellar containing the remains of some flags or banners. These were destroyed and unfortunately there is no description of them. It seems likely that they could have been used on a hired barge on the occasions when these members visited Westminster. No artefacts remain relating to a hired barge.

The Arms of the Spectacle Makers' Company from a window at the Apothecaries' Hall

THE FRAMEWORK KNITTERS' COMPANY (64)

THE ORIGIN of the Framework Knitters does not reach back to the time of the old guilds like so many of the Livery Companies. The first knitted stockings are believed to have been brought to this country by an Italian merchant from Mantua about 1564. These were copied and hand-knitted in silk by the wife of one of Elizabeth I's courtiers. They were offered to the Queen, who thought they were beautiful but too frail to wear. However, she was persuaded to try them and was delighted with the effect. The next advance is a romantic story about a Cambridge graduate called William Lee, who fell in love with a country maiden, who was more interested in her knitting than him. He set about inventing a machine which would make hand-knitting unnecessary. Unfortunately Lee was unable to place his machine on the market and the outcome of his love affair is not known. Lee's successors were more successful in getting the machine accepted and a very profitable industry was set up in London, Godalming and Nottingham. A Fraternity or Company was established and Oliver Cromwell granted the craft a Charter of Incorporation in 1657. Like the Apothecaries, the Company was referred to as a Society by Charles II, when he granted them a new Charter in August 1663 giving the guild powers extending throughout England and Wales. The Company prospered for over a century and indulged in pomp and ceremony, which included a fine Hall, a state coach and a gilded barge with five banners and a band of musicians. Unfortunately, there are no particulars of this barge and no artefacts remaining from processions on the Thames.

The first record of Company arms is in an engraving of 1708. These Arms were not granted and confirmed until 1933. They depict a knitting frame supported by a student of Cambridge University and a female figure representing the country maiden, with the crest of a lamb resting its forefoot on a hank of silk. The motto is 'Speed, strength and truth united'.

In 1769 a Liveryman, J. Sawbridge, became a Sheriff and proceeded to be Lord Mayor in 1775. He was followed by Stephen Sayne, Sheriff in 1773, Sir Charles Flower elected Sheriff in 1799 and Lord Mayor in 1808 and Robert Waithman MP for London elected Sheriff in 1821 and Lord Mayor in 1823. In 1838 when Samuel Wilson, Colonel of the City Militia, a Weaver, was Lord Mayor, Thomas Wood, Framework Knitter, was Junior Sheriff. The Senior Sheriff was Thomas Johnson, a Cooper. The two Companies met at the King's Head Tavern, Poultry at 10.30am on Lord Mayor's Day and proceeded by barge together from London Bridge to Westminster to take their oaths. Gowns and rosettes were worn by the Liverymen.

No artefacts have survived relating to a hired barge.

The Master's Chair of the Framework Knitters' Company
which may have been carried on their Barge

THE WHEELWRIGHTS do not claim any antiquity, they first applied for incorporation in 1631 but their petition was not successful until Charles II granted them a Charter in 1670. This appears to have cost them £300, a large sum in those days. They were granted Livery in 1773. The craft of wheel making was highly skilled and it was important that a wheel should not fail. If a wheel did break down this could cause a considerable delay in the narrow streets of the City as well as damage to the goods being transported.

The Company had four Sheriffs – Robert Peckham in 1777, who became Lord Mayor in 1783; A. Brander in 1792; Sir William Leighton in 1803, who became Lord Mayor in 1806; and George Bridges, MP for London, who became Lord Mayor in 1819. New banners were ordered in 1782. This was the year before Robert Peckham became Lord Mayor and could have been used for his procession on the Thames on Lord Mayor's Day. The banners were the Arms of England, the City and the Company and cost £38 13s. There is a record of the Company hiring part of a barge, when Robert Peckham was sworn at Westminster as a Sheriff in 1777, at a cost of £3 15s 6d. He was Master of the Company in 1800. There are no other records of hiring for these occasions, although those who became Lord Mayor would have processed to Westminster in the City barge. In 1553 members of the Company accompanied Lady Jane Grey to the Tower by barge.

The Company first used Arms in 1682, but these were not approved by the College of Arms until 1965. They depict a chevron between three wheels and an axe supported on either side by a horse and with an arm holding a mallet as the crest. The motto is 'God Grant Unity'.

No artefacts have survived relating to a hired barge.

The Arms of the Wheelwrights' Company

THE WATERMEN'S COMPANY

NTIL the mid eighteenth century London Bridge was the only bridge over the Thames in London. The streets were narrow, crowded and very rough for walking. A boat was therefore important for crossing the river any distance from the bridge. The wherry, a small rowing boat, was also a pleasant and comfortable means of travel from place to place, and boatmen plied for hire in large numbers supplying a service for passengers and cargo. As London grew, it became important that there should be some control and organisation. In 1372 the City authorities established a scale of fares for boatmen on the Thames – for example, the fare from London to Westminster must not exceed 2*d*. An Act to regulate the Watermen was passed in 1514 and a further Act in 1555, which brought the Company into being. In 1559 the scale of fares included passengers travelling between London, Gravesend and Windsor. The Thames had been the main highway for people living and working in London and in 1598 approximately forty thousand men earned a living on or about the river.

The Watermen's Company was granted Arms by Queen Elizabeth. These depict a boat on waves and two oars between two cushions trimmed and tasselled supported on either side by dolphins, with an arm holding an oar erect as the crest. In 1700 the Lightermen, who were formerly members of the Woodmongers' Company, joined the Watermen's Company. The Lightermen were employed in carrying cargo and lightening ships, while the Watermen carried passengers.

As more bridges were built and roads improved there was less demand for the Watermen's trade on the river, while port activities increased and the number of Lightermen became greater. Relief was paid in times of need for loss of income, as when the Thames was frozen over. In the Ordinances of 1626 poor and impotent freemen were to be granted a pension of 8*d* per week. Payments were also made to help wounded freemen returning from the wars. As Watermen and Lightermen were very skilled in handling small boats, they were very much in demand by the Royal Navy. They gave excellent service at sea, in times of danger when the country was threatened by an enemy. The Watermen also helped with fire-fighting, when buildings close to the river caught fire. In this service they often assisted the Insurance Companies. They were also part of the first letter-post delivery service in London.

Freemen who were employed full time by Livery Companies were normally exempt from the Press Gang.

The Companies needed well trained men for the crew of a Livery barge, with a skilled Bargemaster and Mate or steersman. The Doggett's Coat and Badge is awarded to the winner of a sculling race, still held every year from London Bridge to Chelsea which was inaugurated in 1715 by Thomas Doggett, an Irish comedian. John Broughton, a Waterman, won the race in 1730. Later he became the champion prize fighter of England and went on to teach boxing and introduced the first Code of Conduct for boxing. To this day Doggett's wager winners include international class oarsmen.

The Queen still has a Royal Bargemaster, a Freeman of the Company, whose duties are described more fully on page 7. Twenty-three registered Watermen are still appointed by Her Majesty. Their uniforms are kept at St James' Palace. They have duties on certain State occasions and when Her Majesty attends ceremonies connected with the Thames. I believe the first mention of Royal Watermen is when King John travelled by barge to Runnymede to sign the Magna Carta.

A Waterman's badge and licence number, 1820

A Waterman's badge

A Doggett's badge

A model of a Waterman's wherry with a canoe stern

A Waterman's coat and a Doggett's coat

The City Arms from a small barge or wherry,
probably from the vessel's transom

A bargeboard or backrest for the wherry Sarah and Elizabeth

A bargeboard for a wherry belonging to the
Royal and Sunalliance Insurance Group

A bargeboard won as a Regatta prize in 1852

THE OXFORD BARGES

WHEN THE CEREMONIAL processions on the Lord Mayor's Day ceased in 1856 most of the remaining barges belonging to the City Livery Companies were sold. Some had already been disposed of, either because they were no longer in a fit state to be used or on grounds of cost. It was becoming more and more expensive to maintain a luxury used only once or twice a year and very expensive to build a new barge. A large number of these craft were sold by auction and no record was kept of who purchased them. Certainly, five made their way to Oxford, where they were used by the Oxford University Boat Club and the colleges. All five can be traced. Another six barges were to have been bought by Cambridge colleges. They apparently tried to make the journey by sea but were all wrecked on the Norfolk or Suffolk coast. The barges were designed for the Thames, not for going to sea, and would have been difficult to row in rough water. There was very little freeboard and quite small waves could have swamped such craft. However, there does not appear to have been any record in the press of their being wrecked and the exact date of the voyage is not known. It may be that the crew refused the undertaking at the last moment. None of the Livery Companies have any record of their barge being among those that were lost. Fortunately there are some good records left concerning the Oxford barges.

The Merchant Taylors' barge. This was built in 1800 by Roberts of Lambeth for £1,607. The original plans still exist; it was 79ft overall with a beam of 14ft. (Similar plans were used by Roberts for barges for the Skinners, the Clothworkers and the Stationers.) The barge was sold to Oxford University in 1846 for £125. In 1854 it was purchased by University College who kept it until 1873. The next owner of this barge was Wadham College. It was eventually broken up in 1900.

Two photographs, belonging to the University College Archives, give details of the barge. The first, taken in 1872, shows the barge with the College Eight in the foreground. The high lute stern with a platform and seat for the steersman or Bargemaster's mate is shown clearly. This enabled the man at the helm to have a good view over the cabin roof; the Bargemaster would have been in the bow to give directions. Such details were very important in the days when the Livery Companies were processing on the Thames. The long bow, occupied by eighteen oarsmen, shows a very fine hull with very little freeboard. The house or cabin was 30ft long and provided shelter and comfort for the Master of the Company and members of the Livery.

The second photograph taken in 1862 shows the College crew in front of the cabin. The thwarts or seats for the oarsmen and the gang plank can be seen in the foreground. Behind the third crew member on the left is part of a fluted Corinthian column with acanthus leaves. Similar columns are mentioned in the Merchant Taylors' Company archives. The steps to the cabin top or upper deck are probably new, as they take up room on the first seat once occupied by one of the oarsmen.

The Stationers' barge. Searle built this barge in 1826 for £1,785. It was bought by Mr Hall, a boat builder, who hired it to Exeter College in 1849. It was purchased by University College in 1873. There are two photographs of the barge, also belonging to the University College Archives, taken in 1877 and 1878. The first one shows that part of the lute stern has been cut off. The thwarts in the second picture are laminated and very narrow. The Royal Coat of Arms on the cabin roof must have been left behind by the Stationers' Company. This barge was sold in 1879, when the College built a new barge (their third) without a long bow and lute stern.

The Goldsmiths' Company barge, their sixth and last, was built in 1824 by Courthope of Rotherhithe for £1,575. This new barge, with certain modifications, proved to be faster than the other Livery barges and on one occasion overtook the Mercers' barge, a breach in the order of precedence. The number of oars had been reduced from eighteen to sixteen and the rowlocks lowered. The barge had the luxury of a water closet and the steps to the upper deck were inside the cabin porch away from the oarsmen. The decorations were of a very high standard. It is likely that this was the barge bought by Oriel College in 1848 for £100. In 1892 it was rebuilt to a design by Sir Thomas Jackson, the well-known architect, using the same fittings and ornaments which included two carved angels believed to have been on the original barge. The only reference in the Goldsmiths' archives is to an angelic figure designed by Philip Hardwick; there is no record of one or two figures being carved. Two windows with decorations which include a Roman face still survive with the two angels. The barge was eventually broken up in 1954 but several photographs still exist. One which is undated but probably the oldest, taken by Hourse and Taurel of Oxford, shows the typical long bow with eight windows, and part of the lute stern having been cut off. This would have been the part which originally had the carving of a large Coat of Arms belonging to the Goldsmiths. This leaves the transom or main part of hull intact, to which the planks are fitted and on which the rudder hangs. A photograph by Gillman & Soame, also not dated, depicts the reproduction barge of 1893 still with the long bow but the cabin now has ten windows and the steps to the upper deck are inside the porch. The rebuilding and reconstruction of this barge by Sir Thomas Jackson accounts for photographs showing a variation in the number and shape of the windows. The decoration round the windows is the same and two angels are clearly visible.

The Skinners' Company barge. The Skinners' last barge was built by Mr Hall in 1822 and sold back to him in 1858. The Oriel College archives refer to Balliol College owning the Skinners' barge in 1859; later it was sold to Queen's College who used it as their boat house until 1900. During this time it had several extensive repairs. There is a contemporary sketch, partly coloured, which gives good details of the stern, the cabin, the bow and the rowlocks. The artist's name is shown as A. Nibbs.

Other barges. There is no firm evidence as to which Companies the remaining barges belonged or which colleges had an original Livery barge. In his book entitled *Oxford Rowing* (1900), W. E. Sherwood records that in 1857 six Colleges had barges on the river:- Christ Church, University, Exeter, Queen's, Oriel and Brasenose. Unfortunately, the Livery Companies are not named. There is an illustration in Sherwood's book which shows two barges: Oriel on the left and the Queen's on the right. The Oriel barge has eight rounded windows, and Queen's barge has the appearance of the City or Lord Mayor's barge, with Arms on the stern very like the City arms and carving round the cabin top not unlike the model of the last City barge in the Museum of London. It is possible that the fifth barge was the City barge and not that of one of the Livery Companies. This would leave one barge unknown of the six mentioned by Sherwood. Many of the College archives, which could have produced a firm answer, have been destroyed or lost. Perhaps there is an old photograph in someone's attic which would solve the problem.

The next generation of Oxford barges. The University College barge that replaced the Stationers' barge had the advantage of providing the same accommodation for the boat club, without the extra mooring space required for a long bow and overhanging stern. This, the third barge belonging to University College, is now an antique. It is kept, and has been beautifully restored, by Mr David Sherriff, the owner of The Thames and Kennet Marina at Sonning. It was launched in 1883 and was designed by John Oldrid Scott, the architect, and the original drawings are preserved in the Oxford University Boat Club offices. On restoration a small piece of wood was found signed by the original workers on the barge which says 'built by Saunders at Goring and fitted up in Streatley'. (Saunders eventually became Saunders-Roe.)

The later University College barge had no connection with the Livery Companies except in being a decorative and useful house boat with a cabin based on the attractive design of the original Livery barge. It was the beginning of a new generation of barges that were custom-made for Boat Clubs. They were built without the long bow or forward compartment and there was no long overhanging lute stern. This gave more room for changing clothes and storing equipment, and required less mooring space on the river bank. They retained some of the character and appearance of the Livery barges. At one time there were twenty-six of these new – generation barges on the river. A few examples still remain (see Appendix I, page 168).

Oxford Eights Week: the procession of boats in 1858,
with three Livery barges in the background (possibly the
Merchant Taylors', Stationers' and Goldsmiths')

The Merchant Taylors' barge built by Roberts in 1800 and sold
to Oxford University in 1846. University College purchased this
barge in 1854. The photograph shows the College VIII of 1872

The University College Crew of 1862 in the Merchant Taylors' Barge:
(Standing from left) J.E. Parker, F.H. Kelly, A. Makgill, A.E. Seymour, C.N. Gray, J.M. Collyer.
(Seated from left): J.H. Forster, T.W. Gribble, G. Robertson. Note thwarts for the watermen,
the gang plank and the Corinthian column with fluted pillar and acanthus leaves

University College's second barge, the Stationers', in 1877

A model of the Stationer's barge. Note the wheel steering

The University College crew of 1878 aboard the Stationers' barge.
Note the Royal arms are still in place, but the staircase has been built
onto a rowing thwart

The [Goldsmiths'?] barge purchased by Oriel College,
before its reconstruction in 1892

The Oriel barge after reconstruction to a design
by Sir Thomas Jackson, R.A.. The angels on either side of the
porch are clearly visible (see page 156)

One of the two angels from the [Goldsmiths'?] barge

*A photograph of one of the Oriel barge windows
with a detail of part of the lead frame*

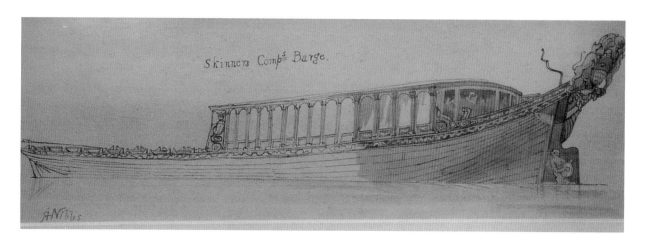

A copy of the sketch of the Skinners' barge by A. Nibbs

*A model of the last Lord Mayor's barge, sold in 1860, for comparison
with the appearance of Queen's barge below*

Oriel and Queen's barges c.1865

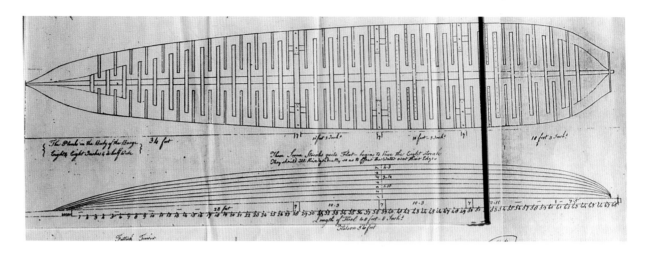

Plans by Richard and Thomas Roberts of Lambeth for the Merchant Taylors',
Skinners' and Stationers' barges c.1800

An engraving showing the type of shallop or small barge
available for hire from Roberts

Purpose-built barges used as College boat houses c.1930

A restoration by David Sherriff of the University College Barge

St John's College barge at Moulsford

BARGEHOUSES

HERE WERE many bargehouses in the area of Lambeth Palace, for which rent was payable to the Palace. Most of the bargehouses had accommodation for the Company Bargemaster. Eleven Livery Companies are known to have had sites which are numbered and recorded on a large map still held in the Palace Library. Besides a site for the Archbishop's own barge, there was a Royal bargehouse next to the Skinners' house and one specified for 'the Prince' (plot no. 24). The Archbishop leased a number of plots of land where bargehouses could be built with access to the river. Some of these can be seen in contemporary paintings of Westminster Bridge, with Lambeth Palace in the background. Among the Companies which made use of these sites were the Grocers' Company who had a lease for twenty-one years at a rent of 10s per annum with 11s 3d land tax. Among other tenants were the Earl Cardigan and the Duke of Norfolk. Both Queen Mary and Elizabeth I visited Lambeth Palace on several occasions by barge. One of the early records of the use of a barge was by Archbishop Pole some time between 1554 and 1558, when he travelled from Gravesend to Westminster and then on to Lambeth Palace at Queen Mary's request. Cardinal Wolsey (Archbishop of York) is known to have had a barge which was used by the Skinners' Company in 1518 when Sir Thomas Mirfine, Skinner, was Lord Mayor. The Archbishop's barge was last used in c.1737 by Archbishop Wake, after which it fell into disrepair; it was rather larger than the average Livery barge, having twenty-eight oarsmen.

At one time the Goldsmiths shared a large bargehouse with the Skinners' Company; however, both moved to land belonging to the Apothecaries at Chelsea in 1656. The Haberdashers rented a bargehouse for £4 per annum. This rent was reduced to 10s with a fine of £20 in 1692. The Pewterers owned a barge in 1662 and shared the Haberdashers' bargehouse. The Ironmongers had a bargehouse close to that of the Barbers who leased land on which they had a bargehouse built by Henry Fforty. This was for the Barbers' first barge in 1662. The Armourers had site no. 125 for which they paid 2s in 1658 for berthing.

The Coopers, whose first of three barges was built in 1683, moved to a bargehouse in Lambeth in the same year. The Vintners rented accommodation there before they moved to Chelsea in 1739. The Merchant Taylors kept a barge at Lambeth but it is not clear if this was on part of the Archbishop's property. The Stationers paid a yearly rent to James Sharpe for a bargehouse with a loft near Lambeth Palace in 1778. The Drapers rented quite a large plot (no. 128) which was 78ft long by 44ft wide and included two small dwellings. One lease was for twenty-one years in 1664 and another lease in 1777 cost £20 per year. From this it is clear that quite a considerable income from these bargehouses was due to Lambeth Palace.

Further down stream from Lambeth, on the same side of the river, just above Blackfriars Bridge, was a bargehouse for Queen Elizabeth's Royal Barge. Forty years ago the oak pile foundations of the slipway could still be seen near a street called Barge House Alley.

The Mercers, the Fishmongers and the Clothworkers had bargehouses at Vauxhall Manor. These were located up river from Lambeth Palace and on the same side of the river. The Tallow Chandlers built two bargehouses on the Apothecaries' property at Chelsea. One of these was sublet to the Weavers' Company and later to the Vintners' Company. The Apothecaries had their own bargehouse next to them.

There must have been a number of barges owned by private individuals and by wealthy firms which had businesses near the river. One example of these is the Phoenix Assurance Company which was one of the original Marine Insurance Companies and insured the Stationers' barge and bargehouse. The Phoenix is known to have lent their barge (which they purchased from the Tallow Chandlers in 1799) to the Clothworkers' Company to process on Lord Mayor's Day in 1803. A barge board with the Phoenix insignia (illustrated on page 149) still exists in the care of the Royal and Sunalliance Insurance Group. This board would have fitted a wherry and was used to support the passengers' backs as the oarsmen drove through the water. The board was decorated to attract custom.

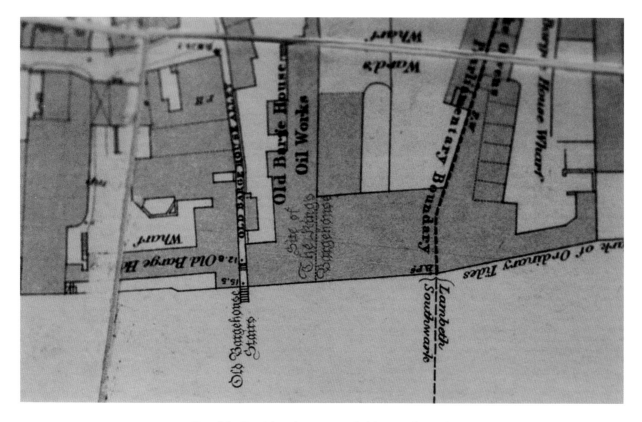

Site of the King's bargehouse, near Blackfriars Bridge on the
South bank of the river, up stream

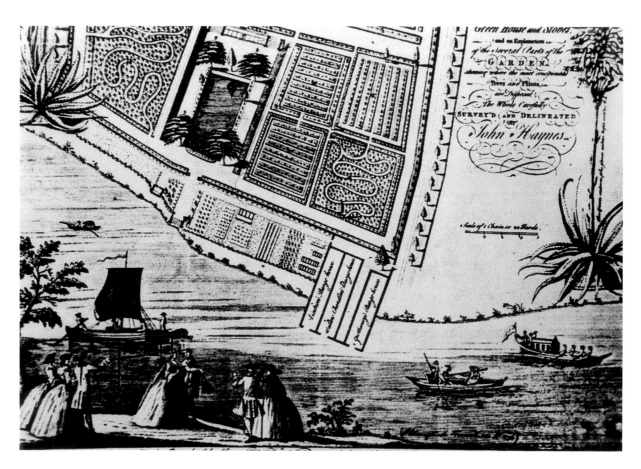

Plan of Chelsea Physic Garden and bargehouses

View of Lambeth Palace by Maurer, 1745,
with bargehouses to the left of the Palace

The Apothecaries' bargehouse at Chelsea c.1856

Searle's boat yard in 1830 with barge houses. The barge stern appears, from the arms, to be that of the City Barge

An oil painting by Pembery shows Searle's boat yard (left) and barges in 1851

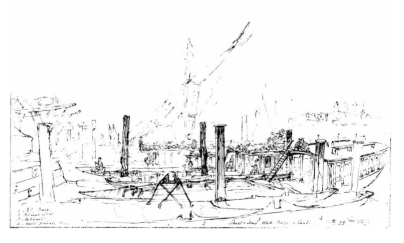

Drawing dated 1849, shows Searle's State Barge Wharf with, from the back, the barges of the Fishmongers, The Stationers and Searle's own private barge

An acquatint dated 1792, by Lord John Henniker, M P, showing Lambeth Palace (right)
and Roberts's boat yard on the left with a livery company barge moored

From a lithograph of 1842 by Radclyffe showing a Westminster
School VIII in front of Roberts's boat yard at Lambeth

THE CITY BARGES AND THE OXFORD CONNECTION
RICHARD NORTON

BY 1826, when the last of the City barges was built, the divergence of interests, which was to change rowing activities on the tidal Thames for ever, had already begun. The condition of the river had deteriorated and bridges had replaced many of the ferries; steam boats were already displacing watermen from their trade. Only a few were able to supplement their living by competing for attractive wagers and many fell on hard times. Amateur rowing was growing up quite separately as a sport in the universities and schools.

By 1822 barges were being used in conjunction with the boat racing on the Isis at Oxford, and it is quite possible that one or more of these had been City barges. In his book *Oxford Rowing*, the Reverend W.E. Sherwood reproduces paintings entitled 'The Eights, 1822' and 'The Eights *circa* 1831' which both show a five-windowed barge with Christ Church Meadow in the background. This is probably [Mr] 'King's Barge' later shared by New College, Pembroke, St John's and Jesus and ultimately acquired by Merton.

In the collection of the London Borough of Richmond upon Thames, a painting of *c.*1840 entitled *Swan upping in Twickenham* and attributed to J.J. Chalon, shows one of the City barges which later went to Oxford (see pages 166-7). A group of spectators on the upper deck are taking the same interest in the proceedings as parties of the Dyers' and Vintners' Companies would in similar circumstances today. The barge is decorated with the figure of an angel at the forward end of the house and there are eight oval windows each side. These are the characteristics of the Oriel College barge as she became in 1848 when she went to Oxford. In 1892 she was rebuilt by Salter Brothers to a design by Sir Thomas Jackson, the architect, who closely followed the original lines, preserving the fittings and ornaments including the gilded angels. The house was lengthened and the eight unusual oval windows with their lead frames were increased to ten each side. Further repairs and embellishments were undertaken in 1921 and again in 1937. It seems more than possible that this was the barge built originally for the Goldsmiths' Company (see page 150).

In 1846, the Lord Mayor's barge was rowed to Oxford on a tour of inspection of the Thames.(The Lord Mayor's barge was popularly referred to as the 'City Barge', whereas the plural of the same expression was a generic term for the City Livery Companies' barges). Her length overall was 75 ft, the house only 29 ft as the space needed was less than in the Companies' barges. On each side of the house there were thirteen windows, and she also had nine rowing positions each side and a sculptured griffin in a recess. There was ornamental work on the upper deck and carving round the City of London arms at the stern. She had been built by Searle at Lambeth in 1807 at a cost of £2,579; some 30-50% more than her contemporaries. A classic vessel of her time, this City Barge was well fitted for her role which was both ceremonial and practical. The Lord Mayor continued to be responsible for the conservation of the River Thames, undertaking regular inspections of the locks and weirs. In the engraving 'The Embarkation at Oxford' which appeared in The *Illustrated London News* of 15th August, 1846, a large party of people, turned out in their finery, are ready to go on board, for the Lord Mayor entertained the civic dignitaries generously (see pages 22 and 176). It was normal on such occasions for the barge to be accompanied by a smaller boat, a 'whiffler', which could act as a tug when necessary. The 'whiffler' would be sent ahead to open the next lock. On this tour the City Barge was accompanied by the Water Bailiff's shallop, seen on the right of the picture.

The last true Lord Mayor's barge was sold in 1860 and then served as The Queen's College barge until 1872 when the college had a houseboat barge built. Evidently, although records are not available from the college, this barge did not prove satisfactory for in 1885 it was decided to buy the Skinners' Barge from Balliol even though this was well past its prime, having been preserved by careful maintenance since the eighteenth century. The college's final solution had to wait until 1908 when the barge which still survives at Binsey was built.

There has been some confusion in the past over the Lord Mayor's Barge, possibly due to the use of the soubriquet 'The City Barge', the misleading fact of the other Lord Mayor's Barge, *Maria Wood*, the lack of records, or undergraduate mistake. The barge in question, however, came to The Queen's College and is illustrated in *Oxford Rowing* opposite page 85. It is distinguished from the Stationers' Barge by the shape of the stern, the griffins and its windows. A question remains: what barge did Queen's own before, when Sherwood noted that in 1857 the barge owners in Oxford were Christ Church, University College, Exeter, Queen's, Oriel and Brasenose?

In 1846 there was a third arrival in Oxford – The Merchant Taylors' barge (see page 152). She was used by the Oxford University Boat Club (founded in 1839) which had hitherto hired a barge from Heather. The Merchant Taylors' barge had been built by Roberts, the King's Bargemaster, in 1800. Subsequently, in 1855, the OUBC commissioned their

own houseboat barge which was designed by E.G. Bruton and built in Oxford. She had gothic features with windows arranged in six triplets. A photograph of her in 1871 emphasises how the sport of rowing and the barges themselves evolved in separate ways.

By the mid-nineteenth century, from being oar-powered mass transport, the barges in Oxford had become prestige rowing headquarters with changing facilities and rafts for access to racing boats, and ferry punts for going across to the tow path. At the same time, technical developments, such as the introduction of light racing shells and sliding seats, were making the sport of amateur rowing even more specialised.

In 1849 the Stationers' Company sold their barge to Mr Hall, the reputedly disagreeable Oxford barge man, who then hired her out to Exeter College Boat Club. She became known as 'The Red Barge' because the window surrounds were painted red and there were two red bands around the edge of the upper deck. These colours were used when she belonged to the Stationers' Company and, co-incidentally, Exeter's colours are also red. In a letter home to his parents written in 1850, Henry Boyd, an undergraduate who rowed in the Exeter 1st VIII that year and who later became Vice Chancellor of the University, describes the scene . . . .

> Well, amidst the cheers of our friends who crowded the top of our barge [the Stationers'], we entered our boat and proceeded down the river in the most

magnanimous manner, all brimful of determination to bump St John's which was directly above us. It was a most exciting sight: at King's barge all the colours of the different boats were flying, one above the other in their order; the banks on both sides were thronged with eager spectators, the bands were playing on the top of the University [OUBC] Barge [Merchant Taylors'], and one boat after another came down to take its position for the races.

[Mr] King's Barge was not one of the City barges, but the five-windowed barge which can be seen in the 1822 and 1831 views in Sherwood's book.

The last Stationers' Barge is described in *The Barges of The Stationers' Company*. There are several photographs in the Exeter College records and more, later ones, in the University College archives. There is a profile photograph of her in Neil Wigglesworth's book *Victorian and Edwardian Boating*, when the staircase to the upper deck was in its transverse position. Contrary to Wigglesworth's assertion, one can be confident that this photograph was taken sometime during the first six years she was in Oxford because the 1856 picture of her in Sherwood's book shows her turned to point downstream with the angels and their trumpets, the thole pins and the ensign staff all removed. As the years passed other changes were made: the decoration was removed from the roof and the high stern was cut down. Built in 1826 by Searle, this barge was the last of the old tradition, with a lute stern rising above the house, thirteen windows each side and one recess. There was decoration

The Stationers' Barge photographed before 1856

The OUBC houseboat barge, built in 1855. This photograph of
1871 shows the winners of the University Pairs: J.W. Mc C.
Bunbury (Brasenose) and A.G.P. Lewis (University College)

This 1873 photograph shows (left) Exeter College's new
barge and (right) the Stationers' (The Red Barge).
In front, the University College IV: from the left:
A.S. Daniell, J.E. Bankes, H.J. Preston, W.P. Johnson

with arms at the forward end and all around the house and
flying angels with trumpets supported the arms at the stern.

As well as this barge, [The Red Barge], used as the home
of the Boat Club, Exeter also had a Green Barge which was
used by the 'barge club'. By 1869 two barges were considered too many but the college authorities were frustrated
by their 'obnoxious' barge man until his demise in 1873.
At last Exeter was able to break from its commitment to
the Red Barge which was moved down one place to the
University College moorings, while Exeter commissioned a

new gothic nine-windowed houseboat barge for the Boat
Club. The Green Barge was then bought by Salters' and
used by St John's.

Meanwhile, in 1872, The University College barge [The
Merchant Taylors'] had become too old and was replaced
by The Stationers' in 1873. From the photographs, we can
see that the new Exeter Barge was moored where the
Stationers' had been, the Stationers' moved down one to
take the place where the Merchant Taylors' had been, and
the latter was probably towed away and broken up, although

The Skinners' Barge (Balliol College) c.1880 (left).
The OUBC Barge (right)

St John's College Barge c.1889

Sherwood, who may have been mistaken, says she went to Corpus Christi.

Today, only nine of the second generation Oxford college barges remain in existence: Queen's at Binsey, Corpus on the Isis, St John's at Sandford under the care of the St John's Barge Limited Charity, Magdalen at Streatley, St Edmund Hall at Reading, University College at the Thames and Kennet Marina, Balliol at Sunbury, Jesus at Richmond and New College at Chelsea. The Hertford Barge was destroyed by a fire started by vandals on 7th July, 1997. She had been awaiting restoration at Sandford by the Trust for Preservation of Oxford College Barges. All these barges have steel or concrete hulls or steel shoes under wood. They are meant to last.

A further note on the Goldsmiths'/Oriel Barge question:

When the Goldsmiths' Company needed a new barge in 1824, they offered a prize for the best design. Philip Hardwick submitted a drawing for an angelic figure but the prize was won by Courthope of Rotherhithe. The cost of the new barge was only £1575.

The Oriel Barge also had the figure of an angel on each side, positioned at the focal point by the entrance to the house, and Oriel College still has the angels. They are the same shape and design as those in Chalon's painting of swan upping referred to earlier. Angels were represented on many of the City barges, but the likelihood that this barge belonged to the Goldsmiths' Company seems more probable because the angels and lead cast oval windows, though delightfully designed features, would have been easy to make, as would the structure to house them, which might account for the comparatively low recorded cost of constructing the Goldsmiths' Barge.

Balliol, Bullingdon and OUBC Barges, date uncertain

New College Barge in 1906

Hertford College Barge, 1911. Principal Boyd wearing the silk hat (below flagpole),
Vice Chancellor 1890, Master Draper 1896

The Jesus College Barge, after restoration, July 1987

MUSIC IN THE BARGES AT THE LORD MAYOR'S TRIUMPHS IN THE SEVENTEENTH CENTURY

JANE PALMER

Based on research undertaken in the archives of the City Livery Companies in preparation for a Ph D thesis
entitled *Music at The Lord Mayor of London's Triumphs, 1604-1708*

The celebration in seventeenth-century London of the Lord Mayor's Triumphs had its roots in King John's Charter of 1215 which required that the newly elected Mayor should be presented at Westminster. For several centuries this ceremony comprised simply a procession from Guildhall, the pageantry and banquet associated with later Triumphs or Shows developing afterwards. Music was a vital ingredient of the swearing-in procession almost from its inception, being used to separate the various components of the procession and to emphasize the grandeur of both the occasion and the participants. It was usual to employ those ceremonial instruments traditionally associated with processions, that is, trumpets, drums, and fifes, which were invaluable in underlining the importance and power of the Livery Companies so closely connected with the event.

From the early fifteenth century, when the Lord Mayor's journey to Westminster was first made by river (rather than on horseback by road), the use of ceremonial barges gradually developed into the most visually spectacular part of the triumphal day. Barges allowed much more scope for lavish splendour with such items as banners, streamers, musicians, water-borne pageants, fireworks, and cannon fire from the shore. An unusual entry in the Ironmongers' Minutes describes the equipping of a galley foist (the usual term for a barge of the Lord Mayor) with '10 peeces of ordinances 16 Musketiers 20 Powers... 3 guners wth powder & Match & all other necessaryes... and ye Comp^s[ny] are to provide 2 drums, 5 trumpeto^{rs} 17 pendants 4 flaggs'.

The barge procession is the best documented part of the day's festivities by onlookers, both in paintings and diaries. Most detailed among literary accounts is that of the 1613 Triumphs written by Horatio Busino, chaplain to the Venetian Ambassador extraordinary in England:

> Scarcely had we arrived when a dense fleet of vessels hove in sight, accompanied by swarms of small boats to see the show like the gondolas about the Bucintoro. The ships were beautifully decorated with balustrades and various paintings. They carried immense banners and countless pennons. Salutes were fired, and a number of persons bravely attired played on trumpets, fifes and other instruments. The oarsmen rowed rapidly with the flood tide, while the discharges of the salutes were incessant.

In contrast to Busino's description, William Nicolson's entry for 1704 from his London Diaries is short and succinct: 'I dined... at Lambeth; whence (the Mist being pretty thick) we had a slender prospect of the Lord Mayor's Cavalcade, by water, to Westminster and the Barges and Streamers that attended him. The Noise of the Guns and Musick (Trumpets, &c.) was more audible, than the shew was Visible.'

The detail reproduced (*opposite*) from a painting in the Royal Collection at Windsor Castle by an unknown Dutch artist of the 1683 Lord Mayor's river procession to Westminster, shows a colourful and lively scene. At least a dozen barges are depicted, each with a group of uniformed musicians playing in the stern, but the only instruments portrayed clearly enough to be identified are shawms and sackbuts. The river is crowded with small rowing boats conveying sightseers, and the numerous landing wharfs and steps are again thronged with people. The flags and banners of each Company adorn their barges and smoke from cannon fire is visible.

Although many of the 'Great Twelve' Livery Companies, and some minor ones too, travelled by barge to Westminster on the Triumphs day regularly from the mid-fifteenth century, their vessels were usually hired, and it was not until the early seventeenth century that Companies began to consider buying their own. Whether or not the Lord Mayor travelled in his own barge or in his Company's barge, the accommodating of those eligible or desirous to accompany him by water was often a problem and it inevitably became common to hire what the Fishmongers described as a 'lesser' barge to accompany the 'greate' barge. Thus it is apparent that, if all the Great Twelve travelled by barge, with three or four of them requiring a second barge, and perhaps half-a-dozen minor Companies made the journey too, it would have been possible to see a full complement of around twenty splendidly decorated barges on the Thames on the Lord Mayor's Day. Furthermore, a large proportion of those barges would have traditionally carried a group of musicians to entertain both the travellers and the onlookers from the shore; no doubt an extraordinary sight and sound. Consequently the number of musicians employed in the barges is likely to be far greater than has previously been thought, when it was assumed that the Lord Mayor's barge was the focus of musical activity.

The day of the Triumphs started early for most participants, as the marshalling of the vast numbers involved in the procession was a lengthy business. The greatest task was faced by the mother Company of the Lord Mayor elect, members of which formed the bulk of the procession, for they were required to escort the Lord Mayor to Guildhall, where the full procession awaited them, and thence to the river for the barge journey to Westminster. Those employed by the Company for the Triumphs, particularly the musicians and the watermen, needed to make an early start, although the following entry in the Haberdashers' special Triumphs Accounts Book seems to be unique in its reference to the trumpeters' meeting time: 'On Monday the xxix[th] of October 1632. The Wardens Assistants and Liverie and all the Batchelors are to meete at the hall by vi of the Clock in the morning and xxxii trumpeters wth their banners to bee at the Lord Maiors by vii of the Clock to bring the Lord Maior to the Guild hall'.

The enforced early start necessitated the provision by the Company of breakfast for many of the participants, but those in employment, particularly musicians, were often given a cash alternative. This payment seems to have been more or less standardized by the second half of the seventeenth century to one shilling per man, irrespective of rank. In 1663 the Clothworkers' Accounts include an entry thus: 'Item paid to the Six Trumpetts that day for their breakfast 12[d] apeece being six in number 6[s.]'. It was more usual to append the cost of breakfast to the fee, as the Goldsmiths did in 1681 for a group of six musicians playing 'on their loud Musique': 'for w[ch] services there was payd unto them 3[li] & more for their Breakfast 12[d] a peece'. Time in which to eat breakfast with the Company would have been short, as music often accompanied the Lord Mayor from his house to Guildhall if he joined the main procession there, and was played more or less continuously in the procession to the Thames, and on the journey by water to Westminster.

The main purpose of gathering either at the Company Hall or at Guildhall was for the grouping into order of all participants in the procession. This order was traditional and never varied, so that everyone including musicians was ranked out two by two into six or seven 'divisions' or groups. The ceremonial instruments associated with processions (trumpets, drums and fifes) were the only ones ever used for the mother Company in the walking procession, although other instruments were often sounded in the barges and for remaining Companies. For example, in 1677 the Goldsmiths, who were not the mother Company that year, made an agreement with 'John Greenslade a Musitioner for himselfe with five others to attend this Company on the next Lord Maiors day wth Hoboyes & Sackbutts from their Hall to the Barge & from there to Westmindster & back againe . . .'. Inferior ranks in the procession, such as pensioners from the Company almshouses, were accompanied only by drums and fifes, while trumpets,

regarded as 'upper class' instruments, played for the superior ranks. Even in years when royalty did not attend the Triumphs, it was customary for members of the King's musicians to attend as required, augmented by the retained musicians of London (the City trumpeters and the City drum and fife), and occasionally drummers and fifers from the Artillery Garden.

The route of the procession to the awaiting barges on the Thames tended to vary in detail but usually went from the Company Hall via the house of the Lord Mayor elect to Guildhall to meet with the former Lord Mayor, and then by the most direct route to the embarcation point on the river. This was the landing stairs at Three Cranes Wharf, which seems to have been used every year, even if the walking route varied. Although the river frontage at this wharf was extensive, it would have been difficult and time-consuming for all the attendant Companies to board their barges from this point, so it is most likely that only the mother Company used Three Cranes, the remaining Companies choosing one or other of the many nearby stairs or wharfs. However, on their return from Westminster, the inevitable delay while all barges discharged their passengers seems to have been acceptable. Once the procession had reached Three Cranes Wharf, those accompanying the Lord Mayor by barge, including musicians, took their places, and the vessels began their slow progress towards Westminster, featuring one of the most celebrated elements of Livery Company life, the order of precedence. Heading the fleet were the Lord Mayor's City barge and the barge of his own Company, followed by those of the Mercers, and the remaining Great Companies in order, allowing for the famous 'sixes and sevens' juxtaposition of the Skinners and Merchant Taylors.

A typical barge of the period that was privately owned by a Company, not hired, would have had a firmly constructed house or shelter amidships, with the oarsmen seated forward in the bows, while the space to the stern accommodated the musicians. Hired barges often had no house, only a barge cloth, or awning, but there would still have been room for musicians. To minimize the discomfort experienced by the travellers, seating was provided in the bargehouse but there is no mention of seats for the musicians: trumpets, fifes and drums were of course quite playable standing up, and it is these that mainly provided music in all barges at first, but even when the choice of instruments expanded later in the century, it would seem that the musicians never sat to play. By standing they commanded more attention but in rough weather this must have been quite an accomplishment. The Tallow Chandlers mention 'the Wetness of the day' in 1664 and 'the Winde being very boistrous' three years later. In fair weather the journey from Three Cranes Wharf to Westminster Stairs took about one hour.

Once the Lord Mayor and those attending him had disembarked at Westminster Bridge no music, not even played by the royal musicians, accompanied the ceremony until their return to the barges for the journey back to the City.

Not all the musicians that walked in the procession to the river wharf would have continued in the Lord Mayor's barge, accommodation in the stern behind the bargehouse being limited. As only certain higher-ranking divisions of Livery Company members made the journey, it is most likely that just the musicians from these divisions would accompany them, while those from the lower ranks awaited the Lord Mayor's return at some convenient gathering place, such as Barnard's Castle, but this is not certain. The pageant pamphlet for 1664 states that only eight of the sixteen royal trumpeters travelled in the Lord Mayor's barge together with the Serjeant Trumpeter and the kettledrummer. Possibly the remaining trumpeters may have joined other Companies' barges. Phrases such as 'Paid to the Lord Maiors Trumpeters' occur regularly in the archives of those Companies known to have travelled by barge, and the fees quoted are more in the nature of a generous tip rather than a full payment. However, trumpeters so employed would certainly not have been the barges' 'only Musick' for there are numerous archival references indicating otherwise. This procedure would have applied solely to the musicians employed by the mother Company, as the remaining Companies, particularly the minor ones, requiring the services of fewer musicians, would have expected them to continue 'as well by land as in the Barge'.

For example, the year 1675 provides us with contrasting details of barge musicians from each of the three groups of Livery Company: the mother Company, a member of the Great Twelve, and a minor Company. Firstly, the Drapers as mother Company ordered that only twelve of the twenty eight trumpeters engaged for the Triumphs were to travel by barge: 'That the Sixteene Kings Trumpetts & 12: others to be brought by them and the Kettle Drumm, do p[er]forme the service of Trumpets the Lord Maiors day; and 12 [replaces the word 'six'] of them to be in ye barges & after with the rest to do ye Land Service'. In the same year, the Goldsmiths, one of the Great Companies but in attendant role only, made an agreement with 'Richard Farmer for himselfe & five sufficient & able persons more to attend the Company in their Barge wth loud musique in consort on the Lord Majors day next from Paules wharfe to Westm[inste]^r and back again'. The use of a group of six players (sometimes five) seems to have been standard for most non-elective Companies, whether minor or members of the Great Twelve.

Finally, in the third example from 1675 the Tallow Chandlers, a minor Company albeit an enthusiastically regular attendant of Triumphs, were offered the services of William Smith, musician, 'to serve this Company on the Lord Majo^{rs} Oath day now next comeing both by Water & Land Wth Loude or Winde Musique and alsoe wth Soft or String Musique; with a Consort to consist of 5 able Music[i]oners besides himselfe'. (In fact, the Tallow Chandlers turned down Smith's offer, believing it to be too expensive.)

The variety of music described in the barges became more extensive from 1658, when the Triumphs finally shook off the shackles imposed by the Civil War and Interregnum. Here we find the first reference to barge instruments other than the faithful drums, fifes and trumpets so often mentioned in the first half of the seventeenth century: 'hoe-boys' and cornets in the pageant pamphlet of 1658 and 'wind-musick' the following year (the latter term is most likely an alternative phrase for a loud consort).

Company archives rarely mention instruments other than the traditional trumpets, drums and fifes so the unusually detailed Tallow Chandlers' records provide invaluable evidence on the instruments used in the later seventeenth century. From 1688 they start to distinguish between two types of music to be hired, both for land and water use, known as loud and small music, or more commonly, wide and still music. While the terms loud and soft were frequently applied to consort instruments, wide, small and still were not in general contemporary use amongst the Livery Companies (although the Blacksmiths use the term 'still' as early as 1616). Here, the contrast of loud and soft music is evident, so that the wide or loud music is to be used in the procession and in the barge, and the small, still or soft music in the more intimate atmosphere of the hall.

In an entry in the Court Minutes for 1670 (apparently unique in Livery Company records), the Tallow Chandlers categorize the instruments expected in such groupings :

> This Courte did alsoe agree with Edward Watts Robert Zmithar and William Morris Musicioners that they together with Henery Duffeild Robert Johnson & one other Able Musicioners shall serve this Company on the Lord Majo^{rs} Oath day now next ensueing (as a Consort) with good Musique both Loude or Wide & alsoe Still Musique and that by land and alsoe by water in their Barge; And the consort of Loude Musique should consist of a Treble hoboy a Double Curtle a Sackbutt and Three Tennor hoboys And that the Consorte of Still Musique shall consist of Three Treble vyolls or Vyolins Two Lutes and a Base Vyall And the Courte did agree to give unto them for their said service the some of iij^{li} land to allow each man vi^d a peece in Steade of a Breakefast

The organization of all aspects of the Lord Mayor's Triumphs was completed in the month between the election of the new Lord Mayor and his swearing-in ceremony. The basic structure of the day stayed the same but the detail varied from year to year and, musically, this meant variance in numbers and names of musicians employed, while payments remained static often for years at a stretch. The mother Company was always accorded the privilege of attendance by royal musicians and the City's own professional musicians, while the other Companies, whether minor or from the Great Twelve, relied on the services of mainly independent musicians of varying ability, although Great Companies could make use of those royal musicians not required by the mother Company. Of the musicians from the Court at Westminster, most essential were the royal trumpeters, led by the Sergeant Trumpeter, and the royal drummers and their Drum Major, with their associated fife players (usually one fife to two, three or four drums). These instrumentalists would be augmented as required by musicians belonging to other royal patrons; it was customary before the Interregnum to hire thirty-two trumpeters and a group usually comprised sixteen players. All were already salaried and liveried, although they traditionally received from the employing Company a gratuity (usually 13s.6d. per man) and certain decorative items for their dress. This fee remains nearly constant throughout the seventeenth century and is most likely to have been a standard participation fee, perhaps to guarantee attendance.

City musicians were either professional or non-professional, the former comprising the City Waits (who were not involved in the barge music, only playing for the pageants and the banquet), the City trumpeters, who numbered about seven, and the City drum and fife. All were engaged and maintained by the Corporation, but payments for additional duties undertaken by the trumpeters came from the employer concerned. Non-professional players comprised independent musicians, possibly of only semi-skilled or amateur status.

Three main options were available for the hiring of musicians, of which most Companies favoured no particular one, using whichever was convenient at the time:

a) Musicians that had served the Company on a previous occasion might offer to play again.

b) Musicians new to the Company might offer their services but the final choice was always left to the Master and Wardens of the Company, in order to maintain some control.

c) This exercising of choice was more easily achieved if members of the Company themselves sought out the musicians. Towards the end of the seventeenth century some Companies started to use the services of a type of co-ordinator to obtain their musicians.

If a musician pleased a Company he was much more likely to be asked to return. A few musicians are known to have been freemen of certain Companies and therefore more likely to be employed by them. It was usual for Companies to offer a greater fee for good service, and also common for musicians themselves to demand what Companies regarded as too high a fee, requiring negotiation.

Musicians engaged for the Triumphs could generally expect to be paid in the week following the celebrations. Musicians connected with the Royal Household or the City's retained musicians commanded a higher fee than independent musicians working in a self-employed capacity. Payments made specifically for musical duties in the barges are scarce but a series of entries recorded by the Goldsmiths show that a varied group of six independent musicians received £2 10s. in the 1660s and early 1670s, rising to £3 in 1677 and £4 in 1688. Payments to all musicians seem to have been fairly standard between Great and minor Companies.

Musicians travelling by barge would have had various types of uniform: the royal musicians and the City's own retained musicians, being salaried, had a livery, while independent musicians usually provided their own version of a uniform up to the Civil War and afterwards would probably have worn mufti). In addition, Livery Companies usually provided salaried musicians with scarves (sashes) and colours (referring to each Company's traditional colours). Ribbon was used to make the latter items, royal musicians usually meriting twice the yardage allowed for City musicians. Trumpeters were nearly always provided with painted cloth banners of the Company's arms for their instruments.

Despite the scarcity of evidence concerning the exact music played and instruments used on the barges there can be no doubt that the river journey to and from Westminster on the Lord Mayor's Triumphs was a cheerful and entertaining affair and only the beginning of what was to be a day enriched by music. The last of the Triumphs in seventeenth-century style took place in 1708, after which the pageants that had customarily followed the procession became unfashionable, despite occasional revivals. However, music was still a vital part of even the most restricted of celebrations, and the river procession remained as colourful as ever. This tradition was upheld throughout the eighteenth and early nineteenth centuries until the setting up of the Thames Conservancy in 1857 forced the Triumphs to abandon the river, reverting once again to a street procession as their predecessors had done over four hundred years earlier.

The [Ironmongers'] Companies Watermens agreement for the Lord Maiors day [1658]

This Writeing Wittnesseth That Whereas wee Robert Frith & Edward Say Watermen; twoo of the owners & constant steers men of Windsor Row Barge, for & in consideration; that wee have receaved of Mʳ William Walter, one of the Wardens of the right Wor[shi]p[fu]ⁱⁱ company of Ironmongers London; Two Blew: Cloakes with Two Sillver Badges of the aforesayd companyes Armes; doe binde our selves, & either of us; joyntly & severaly; unto the right wor[shi]pp[fu]ⁱⁱ the Master & Wardens of that now are, and they or sucksessors, in the some of Twenty pounds, of lawfull mony of England, to performe the condition hereafter written.

The condic[i]on is this; that wee the sayd Robert Frith; and Edward Say; shall and wilbe reddy upon every Lord Maiors day, at Queene hith Stayers in the morneing wᵗʰ a New Row Barge; or a Barge, new trymd up & strowed with greene rushes, with Eight sufficient able men be sides a Greene man; to carry the Master, the Wardens & the rest of the gentlemen, of the clotheing of the said Wor[shi]p[fu]ⁱⁱ company of Ironmongers, to Westminster Bridge; & back againe to Queene hith Stayers; and after they are landed; we are to Carry, up to the sayd Companyes Halle in Fanchurch Street; all such chayer furniture; wᶜʰ the sayd Company useth for chayer accomoda- tion; in and about yᵉ Barge, and at the delivery ther of; the sayd company is to pay unto us the som of Five pounds, & six shillings of lawfull mony of England; & a dinner, such as the sayd Wor[shi]p[fu]ⁱⁱ Company shall think fit. And for to continiu yearly, for the Terme of Twenty & one yeares; after the date hear of; if we or either of us shall for long live; In Witnesse whereof, wee have here to set our hands & seals; this twenty eight day of October; one thousand six hundred fifty eight

Signed Sealed & delivered; in the presence of us.

Robert Skrine   Robart Frith

Will: West

Henry Gifford   Edward Say

THE BARGE FLAGS OF THE CITY LIVERY COMPANIES

The flags which the Lord Mayor and livery companies used in their barges were picturesque. Flags are, after all, of fundamental significance in war and peace, symbolising the identity and allegiance of the vessel and the crew. These flags dramatically represented the powers of heaven and earth, St George, St Paul, the patron saint of the company, the Sovereign, the Lord Mayor, and the Company, and so were particularly impressive.

The Lord Mayor is accorded the courtesy title Admiral of the Port of London. The barges were his fleet. The Navy was augmented in time of war by any ships from the Thames which could be requisitioned, or built in time. Just as in the Navy the ships of a squadron wore the ensign of their admiral, so the flags which the Lord Mayor was entitled to fly were displayed in the companies' barges. In 1354 the Lord Mayor was granted a Royal Charter conferring on him the privilege of having a mace borne before him "… gold or silver, with the sign of our arms" − by implication this could be extended to the use of the Royal Standard as a flag as well. The arms have been altered many times over the years, with extra lions; they have been impaled with the ancient Scottish standard, and the French and Welsh symbols have been added: such alterations are reflected in the various paintings of the barges − in which the following customary uses were observed:

At the bows: The Royal Standard.

On the deck-house, a short staff for each:
The Arms of the City of London. These consist of a St George's Cross, red on white, with the Sword of St Paul in the first canton.
An image of St Paul, gold on red.
The flag depicting the patron saint of the Company.
The Company's crest.
The Union flag, which itself changed over the years.
There were sometimes additional pennants.

At the stern:
The Company's insignia displayed as a carved crest across the lute boards at the stern. They are also represented in a flag flown like an ensign.

In the orders or instructions for the processions it was often required of the companies to bring out from their halls their flags, ensigns, streamers, and the pennants with little bells which completed the effect.

In examining the paintings of the barges, the flags can be difficult to identify. An artist may change his convention when painting flags as he does with lettering, and adopt a more impressionistic style, to avoid too much eye-distract- ing realism.

See Carr, C. 'Barge flags of the livery companies' from the *Mariners' Mirror* Vol 28, No 3, July, 1942

THE LORD MAYOR'S VIEW OF THE RIVER:
OXFORD TO HAMPTON COURT

FROM *THE ILLUSTRATED LONDON NEWS* OF 15 AUGUST 1846

'Upon the proposal of the Visit the Ceremonial was loudly objected to on the score of the great expense. In 1826 "it was said" each Alderman invited two ladies; in 1839 the same authority also invited two ladies and the Lord Mayor an unlimited number of guests, besides giving a dinner and ball at Windsor...'

'Sir Peter Laurie moved in the Court of Aldermen that the expenses be limited to £150.' In 1839 Alderman Wilson, who merely went so far as Henley, had spent £1,000. Sir Peter contended that the authorities had no business beyond the boundary-stone at Staines. 'Alderman Musgrove moved that only Aldermen and Sheriffs should make the excursion. Both motions were negatived, the latter, however, by one vote only!'

On 5 August the Lord Mayor gave a Banquet, with many speeches, at the Star Hotel, Oxford.

'On 6 August the Civic Party rose early and embarked at Folly Bridge. The banks of Christ Church Meadow, and every spot from which the embarkation could best be seen, was crowded with spectators, who loudly cheered the visitors. The morning was bright and the State Barge, with its splendidly emblazoned scarlet silk banners, waving in the sunbeams, had a most brilliant effect, whilst the official import of the occasion was denoted by the City Marshal bearing his mace, and the Royal Standard waving at the bow of the richly carved and gilded craft. The great barge was followed by the shallop of the Water Bailiff, rowed by eight watermen. In another boat, provided with an awning was the military band of the West Essex Yeomanry; and, in a third boat, was the Lord Mayor's Household, who had charge of the provisions for the Civic Party: and a goodly freight it was of cases of wines, delicious fruits, etc.'

'At a quarter past eight the gay flotilla departed amidstloud cheering, firing of salutes, and the enlivening music of the band.'

Horses soon took charge of the Barge, it seems. At Benson Lock two horses fell into the river. Strong men pulled them out: and 'the Lord Mayor generously rewarded the rescuers by giving them a sovereign'.

At Streatley, carriages took the party to Basildon Park, the seat of James Morrison, Esq, MP. He gave them a Banquet which 'comprised turtle and venison and every delicacy', followed by speeches and 'a superb ball'. Thus 'the portion of the river between Streatley and Reading was not surveyed by the entire party'.

At Reading, though, 'shortly after eight o'clock on the 7th the Civic Party assembled at High Bridge, Reading, where they were greeted by a large company, who were stationed in a barge on the Kennet, gaily decorated with flags and garlands of flowers, and enlivened by a band of music. A salute of maroons was also fired; the Civic Party threw coin among the people and then re-embarked, accompanied by the Mayor of Reading and his family. The morning was unfortunately hazy, and threatened rain...'

'At Cliefden Spring, where the Civic Party landed for a short time, the Vintners' Company were dining, it being their annual excursion day to mark the cygnets...'

'The Civic Party withdrew to the saloon of the State Barge to partake of an elegant banquet... There were speeches again, and the Lord Mayor, replying to the toast of his lady, 'expressed his regret that the Lady Mayoress was so bad a sailor that he could not persuade her to come upon the water. Her Ladyship followed them en route as near as she could by land; he expected to find her at Windsor...'

Speeches continued and the Lord Mayor was giving 'the Health of Mr Leach, the Corporation Surveyor' when 'the ringing of bells, the shouts of the multitudes that lined the banks, and the firing of cannon, announced that the party had safely arrived at Windsor.' The banquet had lasted for nine river miles.

On Saturday, the 8th, the party embarked at nine o'clock 'under a salute of maroons, and a company of Life Guards on the river bank'.

At the City Boundary Stone, at Staines, 'an olden ceremony was performed'.

'The State Barge being moored close to the edge of the meadow, the Civic Office bearers embarked and with the Lord Mayor, Aldermen and Sheriffs, grouped around the Stone. Alderman Moon then ascended to its summit, and there drank "God Bless the Queen and Prosperity to the City of London". Three cheers were given; the band played "God Save the Queen", cake and wine were distributed among the party, and small coin was thrown among the crowd.'

'There is an old custom of bumping at the Stone the Sheriffs and Aldermen who have not been made "Free of the Waters"; accordingly, four Watermen seized upon Sheriff Laurie, and while they were bumping the "worthy Sheriff" his colleague, Sheriff Chaplin, made his escape... Upon Alderman Moon descending from the Stone he was instantly bumped... Those who had been so served then paid certain fees, and were declared Free Watermen of the River Thames...'

'At Hampton Court "the Civic View" terminated, the company leaving the State Barge to partake of a banquet prepared for them on board the *Maria Wood*, moored off Hampton Court Palace.'

[*See pages 22 and 23*] 'THE LORD MAYOR AND THE CITY BARGES'

CHRONOLOGY

1189	First Mayor of London.
1215	Charter granted by King John gave Londoners the right to elect their Mayor annually and stipulated that the new Mayor should be presented to the Monarch at Westminster.
1319	Charter granted by Edward II established that only guild members could be freemen of the City of London.
1393	Statute confirmed giving conservancy of the River Thames, from the Staines Bridge to the Medway, to the Corporation of London.
1415	A procession on land and water to welcome Henry V on his return to England after his victory at Agincourt.
1422	Funeral procession of Henry V.
1429	Coronation of Henry VI.
1453	First Livery barge built to order.
1487	Coronation of Henry VII and his Queen, Elizabeth of York.
1509	Funeral procession of Henry VII.
1515-16	Order of precedence of Livery Companies settled by special Court of Aldermen.
1533	Anne Boleyn married to Henry VIII. Processed from Greenwich to the Tower of London en route for her coronation, accompanied by the Lord Mayor and citizens. The Lord Mayor's barge, which was bedecked with banners and streamers, was preceded by a great dragon casting wild fire and making hideous noises in order to clear the way.
1536	On the occasion of a grand tournament at Greenwich Palace, Queen Anne was, by order of the King, arrested and conveyed in her barge to the Tower where she was later tried and executed.
1540	Anne of Cleves processed from Greenwich for her marriage.
1553/4	Lady Jane Grey taken to the Tower by water and later executed.
1603	Queen Elizabeth I's body conveyed by barge to Whitehall where she lay in state for a month.
1662	Procession of over 1000 barges and boats, including two gondolas presented by the Doge of Venice, to greet Catherine of Braganza on her arrival in London to marry Charles II.
1666	Great Fire of London.
1750	The first Westminster Bridge completed.
1769	The first Blackfriars Bridge completed.
1806	Funeral of Admiral Lord Nelson. His body was conveyed by barge from Greenwich to the Admiralty at Whitehall, flanked by eighteen row boats and followed by the Lord Mayor's barge and those of eight Livery Companies.
1815	The tow-barge of the Corporation of London, the *Maria Wood*, was commissioned, 140ft long by 19ft beam, with a saloon 56ft long that could seat 140 for dinner; cost £3,300.
1849	The Coal Exchange opened by HRH Prince Albert. The Lord Mayor and officials in the City Barge embarked at Southwark and proceeded to Whitehall where a procession was formed. The steamboats of the Skinners, the Drapers and the Watermen and Lightermen were stationed below London Bridge, while the barges of the Fishmongers, Grocers and Mercers were stationed on the south side. The procession was witnessed by many thousands, every house, wharf and bridge along the river being crowded with spectators.
1856	The last Lord Mayor's procession on the River Thames.

GLOSSARY OF TERMS

Banner	A type of flag usually hung from the top edge on a horizontal pole, but often applied to any flag used on ceremonial occasions on a barge, or in processions on land.
Barge	Ceremonial state vessel or flat-bottomed coastal trading vessel.
Barge cloth	A cloth forming a canopy over the centre part of a barge to provide shelter for the passengers.
Beadle	A Livery Company officer, one of whose duties is acting as mace-bearer
Beam	The width of a vessel at its widest part.
Clinker	A method of boat building used for small craft where the lower edge of the external planks overlaps the upper edge of the one below, fastened with clenched (riveted) nails.
Court	The governing body of a Livery Company.
Draught	The amount of water required to float a particular boat. This is usually marked on the bow of large vessels.
Earnest	Money paid as an instalment to confirm a contract.
Festones	Hanging chains of flowers carved in wood. (Festoons).
Freeboard	The distance from the water line to the deck or the top of the side of a boat.
Heraldry	Heraldry plays an important part in the history of the City Livery Companies and nearly always provides a clue to the origin and purpose of the Company. It originated in the Middle Ages as a means of identification when most people were unable to read. It was used at first on shields to distinguish persons and properties.
	(For those interested in the full description of the Arms of the Livery Companies there is an excellent publication *The Armorial Bearings of the Guilds of London* by John Bromley and Heather Child.)
House	The cabin on a barge.
Kirtle	A petticoat.
Liberalitas	Mythical figure representing kindness, generosity, bounty.
Lute, lute stern	A high stern on a barge, developed to improve the helmsman's view; so called for its likeness to the shape of a lute.
Mark	A medieval token in the form of a gold or silver weight, worth 13s 4d in England in 1450.
Mortmain	The condition of lands held inalienably by corporations.
Mystery	The archaic name for a handicraft or a group of people carrying out that craft.
Pennant	A long banner or flag, usually about 3ft at the hoist and 15ft long, tapering to a point.
Pietas	Mythical figure representing plenty, duty to family and country, affection.
Preat	A small flag.
Quarterage	A purse for containing the Company's dues, collected every quarter.
Rooler/Rooling pin	Used to rod or roll a flag on for storing when not in use.
Rowlock	Shaped space cut in the boat's gunwale or side in which an oar works, or levers. Also a metal crutch used for the same purpose in smaller rowing boats.
Saxboard	The uppermost plank forming the side of a boat, usually heavier than the other planks and carrying the rowlocks.
Shallop	A small boat usually rowed by two to six men, although Queen Mary's Shallop had eight oarsmen.
Streamer	A small pennant.
Sweep	A long oar with narrow blade worked by an oarsman sitting or standing on a barge.
Taffrail	A rail at the stern of a ship, usually carved with an ornament.
Thole pin	A wooden peg, used instead of a rowlock, usually in pairs or with a rope loop round one pin to secure an oar for rowing.
Thwart	A transverse wooden seat for the oarsman in a rowing boat, supported by wooden knees attached to the side of the boat and a keelson (or other support) from the keel.
Tilt-boat	A small boat with a tilt or cloth canopy to shelter two or three passengers.
Trail board	A carved board at the head of a ship to support the figurehead.
Trundle	Container for gold thread
Wharf	A platform or quay to which a ship or barge can be moored to unload its passengers or cargo.
Wherry	A small vessel with a long sharp stem used for carrying passengers and their baggage, usually propelled by one sculler, or two oarsmen.
Whiffler	A small boat to help clear the way for Livery Barges, usually used as a ferry boat.

BIBLIOGRAPHY

Secondary Sources

Allderidge, B. and Anne Petrides, *State Barges on the Thames*, London, 1959

Allison, Ronald and Sarah Riddell (eds), *The Royal Encyclopedia*, London, 1991

Blackham, R., *The Soul of the City: London's Livery Companies*, London, 1931

Cave-Browne, J., *Lambeth Palace and its Associations*, Edinburgh and London, 1882

Gardiner, Dorothy, *The Story of Lambeth Palace*: a historic survey, London, 1930

Hazlitt, W. Carew, *The Livery Companies of the City of London*, London, 1892

Kemp, Peter (ed.), *The Oxford Companion to Ships and the Sea*, London, 1976

Lang, Jennifer, *Pride without Prejudice: the story of London's guilds and livery companies*, London, 1975

McNarry, Donald, 'Livery Barges of London', *Model Shipwright* no. 82

Murdoch, Tessa, 'The Lord Mayor's Procession of 1686: the Chariot of the Virgin Queen', London Middlesex Archaeological Society, vol. 34, 1983, pp 207-212

Norton, Peter, *State Barges*, National Maritime Museum, London, 1972

Osborne, Michael, *The State Barges of the Stationers' Company 1680-1850*, London, 1972

Rowntree, Diana, 'Oxford College Barges', *The Architectural Review*, July 1956

Sayle, R. T. D., *The Barges of the Merchant Taylors' Company*, London, 1933

Sherwood, W. E., *Oxford Rowing, a history of boatracing at Oxford from the earliest times*, Oxford, 1900

Primary sources

The Royal Archives, The Royal Collection Trust, Windsor Castle

Archives of the Corporation of London

Archives of the Livery Companies at the Guildhall

The Guildhall Library

The Library of Oriel College, Oxford

The Library of University College, Oxford

The Textile Conservation Centre, Hampton Court Palace (banners in store or under repair)

The Transport Museum, Covent Garden

The Victoria and Albert Museum

Archives and artefacts at the Livery Company Halls

The Lord Chamberlain

Mr Norman Dix, formerly of University College, Oxford

Dr John Parry, Oriel College, Oxford

Mr David Sheriff, Caversham

Turk's Boatyard

Mr John Wolstenhome, University College, Oxford

LIST OF SUBSCRIBERS

Sir Timothy Ackroyd, Bt
Andrew J.C. Adams
John G. Adams, F.C.A., A.C.M.A,
    Past Master of the Company of
    Watermen and Lightermen
Michael Adams
Dr Donald Adamson, J.P.
Nicholas Rolfe Adlam
John S. Allan
Charles Alexander, Merchant Taylor
David Allen
H.J. Allen
Claire Angier
The Worshipful Society of Apothecaries
Francisco Javier Aresti
R.A.H. Arnold, Past Prime Warden,
Shipwrights' Company
Mr and Mrs H.G. Ashton
Mrs Iris Austerberry
Professor Anthony Charles Bailey
Nicholas Bailey, Upper Warden,
    Wax Chandlers' Company
Dr Anthony Balfour
Keith F.C. Baker
Mr and Mrs Richard Barker
John Sharer Barkes
A.R. Batchelor
J.H. Bateman
C.G. Bazeley
T. Beedham, F.R.C.O.G., Apothecary
Sir Christopher Benson
Christopher Berry Green, Vintner
Nick Birch, Waterman and Boatbuilder
Charles Birts
Skiff Admiral of Upper Thames
Roger Blackburn
Richard B. Blaxland, Wax Chandler
Peter and Rachel Bleackley, mv *Accolade*
Martin and Margaret Boissier
Peter F. Booth, F.C. Optom.
Jonathan F. Braby
Lord Braybrooke
J.R. Brett
Alderman David Brewer
Dr M.C. Brough
Arnold Phillipps Brown, Fishmonger
Geoffrey and Patricia Brown
Ronald Buchanan
Alan G. Burgess, Galbraith's Limited
The Revd Henry K. Burgin, F.R.S.A.
Yvonne M. Burley
Arthur Burnand, F.R.I.C.S.
Sir David Humphery Burnett Bt
T.J. Burslem
Colonel Michael Burton
David Butler-Adams
Dr R. St J. Buxton
Peter Byrom
Scrivener Mervyn Leonardo de Calcina-Goff,
    A.S.I.S., F.R.P.S., F.S.E.E., F.B.P.A.
Sir Peter Cazalet, Tallow Chandler
Alderman Sir John Chalstrey
Lt Colonel R.W.C-Charlton, O.B.E.
Gerald Charrington

R.Chester-Browne
07000 City Venues
W.O. Clark
Worshipful Company of Clothworkers
Maurice D. Cocking, Tallow Chandler
Andrew Cockrill, O.I.
Oliver Colthurst, Goldsmith
Charles Kevin Connolly, T.D., M.A., F.R.C.P.
Hugh Constant, Apothecary and Waterman
Robert Copeland, Liveryman of the
    Goldsmith's Company, Potter, Author
    and Lecturer
Worshipful Company of Cordwainers
Corporation of London Records Office
John J. Cox
A.M.A. Crawford
R.Guy H. Crofts
R.G. Crouch, Bargemaster to
    H.M. The Queen
J.G.P. Crowden, K.St J., J.P., Past Master
    of the Company of Watermen and
    Lightermen
Royal & Sunalliance Insurance Group
Dr William J. Currie
Dr S.E.T. Cusdin, Apothecary
Walter and Heather Cutting
Peter D.S. Dale
David B. Dalladay
Dr Kenneth Day, F.R.C. Psych.
Mrs Judith Deakin
Alan Dickinson, F.C.A., Chartered
Accountant and Shipwright
Lt Colonel and Mrs John Dingwall
J.F. Doble
Richard Drake, Vintner
Maldwin Drummond, O.B.E., J.P., D.L.,
    Hon D.Sc.
Daphne Ducker
Cdr G.C.M. Dunbar, R.D.★★, R.N.R.
Dr Robin Durance
Denise and Peter Durrant
Mark Edwards, Boatbuilder
Thomas G.Ellison, Spectacle Maker
Philip J. Emerton, Wargrave, Berks
Alistair Farley
P.R.K. Fender
Dr I.T. Field, C.B.E., Senior Warden,
    Society of Apothecaries
Professor Peter Flute
Lorimer Fison
Walter John Ford, I. Eng, F.I.E.D.
D.W. Fuller
W.G.H. Fuller
Elizabeth Fulton, Cirencester, Gloucestershire
Donald B. Fraser
Peter and Mary Fraser
Peter Gardner, Stationer
Edwin and Joyce Gifford
A.J. Gillett
Worshipful Company of Girdlers
Worshipful Company of Glaziers
J.E. Godrich
Mrs M.C. Goldman
Michael W. Goold, Saddler

Vincent P. Grant
Anthony Green, Tallow Chandler
Colin S. Griffin, Master Cooper
Andrew Grima, Jeweller
Robert J. Grimer
G. Grosvenor
J. Guiton
Ms Elizabeth M. Hale
Ian K. Hall
John Hall, Merchant Taylor
P. Hames, Clerk, Stationers' Company,
    1984-96
Christopher Harrold, M.A., C. Chem.,
    F.R.S.C.
John G.M. Hart, M.A.
Mrs Iris Haslam, D.St J.
R. H. Hamel Cooke, Owner, Restorer,
    Queen's Barge, Port Meadow, Oxford
Thomas W. Harrison
Michael Harvey, Master, Worshipful
    Company of Wax Chandlers
Surgeon Captain J.R. Haydon, F.F.O.M., R.N.
C.F. Hayman
Henley Royal Regatta
Colin Henwood
Mr and Mrs R.G. Godsland
Miss K.M. Higley, B. A. M. A.
Miss R. Higley, B. Sc.
Ian S. Hill, M.S., F.R.C.S.
T.D.D. Hoffmann
Chancellor J. L. O. Holden
Diana and Geoffrey St John Hollis
Ian Hope-Morley
K.M. Howe
Tony Howitt, Past Master, Merchant
    Taylor's Company
B.P. Hughes, Tallow Chandler
Keith Hutton, Stationer
Cecil Humphery-Smith, Broderer and
    Scrivener
K. Hylton-Smith, Leander Club
R. Hylton-Smith, Leander Club
Brand Inglis
Worshipful Company of Innholders
Ipswich School
Anthony J. Jackson, J.P.
Donald Jackson, M. V.O.
Edward A. Jackson, Wheelwright and
    Waterman
Michael M.O. Jodrell
John Andrew Jupp, Honorary Waterman
    to The Museum of London
Mrs Carolyn M. Kelly
O. Khan
Chris King, Past Master, The Cordwainers'
    Company
Oliver J.R. Kinsey
Dr Paul Knapman
F.A. Knights
S. Kroes
J.B.N. Kurkjian, Master, Worshipful
    Company of Tallow Chandlers
Langford's Marine Antiques
P.C. Laurie

Edwin and Fiona Lawrence
Mrs Rosemary F. Lewis
Richard Ling
P. A. Lingard, C.B.E., T.D.
Christopher J. Livett
David Llewellyn
David A. Longbottom
Sir Ian Lowson, Bt
David Lunn-Rockliffe
His Honour Robert Lymbery, Q.C., M.A.,
    LL.B.
J.St C. Mc Cormick, F.R.C.S. Ed.
Ian A. MacRae
John Marsh
Eric Marshall
Alex Martin
Miles G. Maskell
Peregrine Massey, Merchant Taylor
Mrs Joyce Meade
Merchant Taylors' School, Northwood
William Meredith-Owen,
    New College Barge, Old Ferry Wharf,
    106, Cheyne Walk, London S.W.10
Dr Roger LL. Meyrick
John R. Millard
D.G. ('Tiny') Milne, C.B.E.
John Minter, C.B.E., D.L.
A.J.B. Missen, J.P., M.D., F.R.C.S., Master,
    Worshipful Company of Barbers
Mrs Susan Mitchell
Richard Model
Dennis Monckton
David I. Moor
Colonel G.C.P. Morgan, D.L.
Dr R. Morley, Northumberland
Dr C.A. Morris, M.D., Apothecary
Joan Mossman
The Venerable John Morrison
Congratulations from your 2 i/c
    10 Field Ambulance
Worshipful Company of Musicians
The Museum of London
Hambleden Sales and Charter
Captain Derek W. Napper, C.B.E., R.N.
Mrs P.J. Nason
J.A.S. Neave
Colonel F.G. Neild
Martin Neville
Chas G. Newens
D.F. Newman, Carpenter and Waterman
    and Lighterman
Jeremy D. Nicholson
Dr K.H. Nixon, Apothecary
R.A. Norman-Smith, Fishmonger
R.B. Norton, Draper
Dr and Mrs C.H. Nourse
Simon M. Nutbrown
Charles O'Leary
Peter and Judy Olliff
David, Michael and Mrs Betty Orvis
Pamela Page
James and Edward Palmer
Mr and Mrs J.W.N. Palmer
Dr R. Parker
C.G. Parsons
John Parkhouse, Goldsmith
Dr J. Parker-Williams
John Meredydd Parry, O.B.E., K.St J.,
    M.B., F.R.C.S., F.R.C.G.P.

R. Grant-Paton, Stationer
John Paul
Roger Peel, F.R.C.S. (Edin.), F.R.C.O.G.
Maurice Arthur Phelps
Roger Pincham, CBE, in memory of
    Danny Hick
Gordon S. Planner, Past Master, Wax
    Chandlers' Company
Port of London Authority
Dr Ian Prentice
Rina P. Prentice
Mrs M.C. Prior, J.P.
The Revd and Mrs A. Pryse-Hawkins
R.C. Pulley, J.P., F.C.A.
Dr Norman Pollitt
Nigel Pratt
Cecil H. Rapport, C.B.E., K.St J., J.P., D.L.,
    Horner and Welsh Livery Guild
Nicholas Reed, Lilburne Press
J.L. Reed, M.B.E., M.A., Cooper and Barber
Dominic Reid, the Pageantmaster
John Esmond Rees, M.D., F.R.C.P.
Michael C. Pereira-Rego
John Rew
P.T. Rippon, J.P., D.L., Past Master,
    Stationers Company
River and Rowing Museum Foundation
Chris Roberts
Peter D.T. Roberts
Mrs Eric Robinson
Miss Ruth J. Roe
Mr and Mrs L.R. Roerig
William and Penelope Rose
M.E. Rotheram, Goldsmith
Dr Robert Rowe, C.B.E.
Colonel Sir John Ruggles-Brise
Jennifer E. Rusby
Worshipful Company of Salters
James M. de Santos
George M. de Santos
J.A. Schilling
John Scott
Mrs Sarah Scott Johnston
R. Sergeant, F.R.C.S.
John and Sharman Sheaf
Rasher Skelton and Eggs Skelton
Worshipful Company of Scriveners
David and Nora Scrutton
T.H. Seager Berry
Liveryman Clive Sharples
C.E.Sheppard
David and Clare Sherriff
Worshipful Company of Shipwrights
Patrick Shorten, Stationer
Dr P.D. Simmons
Tom W. Skeels
Worshipful Company of Skinners
Martin Slocock, Chairman, St John's
    College Barge Ltd
Dr Richard Smith
Michael J. Snyder, F.C.A., Deputy
John South, Liveryman and former Beadle
    of The Merchant Taylors' Company
W.F.W. Southwood
Michael D. Spear
Nigel and Wendy Spearing
The Worshipful Company of Spectacle Makers
Duncan Spence

Christopher W. Sprague
L.R. Springett, Baker
S.E.A. Spong, Past Master Watermen's
    Company, 1980/81
The Stationers' Company Library
John Stevens
Roger Stollery
Lord Strathcona, Fishmonger
R.J. Stringer
Michael Sutcliffe
Mr and Mrs P.D. Symons
C.C. Taylor
Mrs Enid Taylor
James F. Tearle
Mrs V.M. Thomas, Freeman
Richard B. Thorpe
John Harcourt Topham
Gwendoline Tough
Peter and Betty Train
R.W.G. Threlfall
P.Q. Treloar
H.E. Tune, C. Eng., F.I.M.E., F.R.I.N.A.,
    F.C.M.S., Liveryman and Shipwright
Captain F.J. Turk, M.V.O., M.N. (retd)
Richard G. Turk
Geo. W. Tutt, Freeman of the River
John and Judy Tydeman
Lord Vestey
Worshipful Company of Vintners
Mrs Lena Walsby-Tickle, Liveryman of
    the Spectacle Makers' Company
Sydney Waissel
Michael Ward, Master, Society of
    Apothecaries, 1993-4
Dr and Mrs Harold W.C. Ward
H. Richard Walduck, J.P., M.A., Basketmaker
Alexander H.E.P. Walduck, B.A., Basketmaker
Simon M.Carruthers, B. Sc.
Worshipful Company of Watermen and
    Lightermen
Dr B.M. Watney
Peter H. Watkins
Ronald Watts
Richard Way
Dr Michael A. Weller
Thomas Whipham, C.B.E.
M.H. White
Mrs G.D. West
Roger West
Jay Whitcombe
D.E. Wickham, M.A., A.R. Hist. S.
Thomas Bain Willcox
Sir Graham Wilkinson, Bt
Brian Williamson
A.R. Willis
R.T.D. Wilmot
Michael Wilmot
Nigel H. Wingate
A.C. de Winton
Peter Wilson
P.J. Wood, F.C. Optom.
A Family Friend
Dr G. Woodbine
Frank W. Yeomans

INDEX

Note: bold type indicates main references

THE LIVING TRADITION

The shallop, Royal Thamesis, *commissioned by the Thames Traditional Boat Rally committee to celebrate the Rally's twentieth anniversary, was built by Michael Dennett of Laleham and his son Stephen Dennett who carried out all the carving.* Royal Thamesis *was launched at Henley-on-Thames on 19th July, 1997. The design is based on the Queen's Shallop or Royal Barge of 1689 (see pages 12 and 13)*